EGYPTIAN TALES

TRANSLATED FROM THE PAPYRI

FIRST SERIES
IVth TO XIIth DYNASTY DYNASTY

EDITED BY
W. M. FLINDERS PETRIE,
HON. D.C.L., LL.D.
EDWARDS PROFESSOR OF EGYPTOLOGY, UNIVERSITY
COLLEGE, LONDON

INTRODUCTION

It is strange that while literature occupies so much attention as at present, and while fiction is the largest division of our book-work, the oldest literature and fiction of the world should yet have remained unpresented to English readers. The tales of ancient Egypt have appeared collectively only in French, in the charming volume of Maspero's "Contes Populaires" ; while some have been translated into English at scattered times in volumes of the "Records of the Past." But research moves forward ; and translations that were excellent twenty years ago may now be largely improved, as we attain more insight into the language.

For another reason also there is a wide ground for the present volume. In no case have any illustrations been attempted, to give that basis for imagination which is all the more needed when reading of an age and a land unfamiliar to our ideas. When following a narrative, whether of real events or of fiction, many persons--perhaps most--find themselves unconsciously framing in their minds the scenery and the beings of which they are reading. To give a correct picture of the character of each of the various ages to which these tales belong, has been the aim of the present illustrations. A definite period has been assigned to each tale, in accordance with the indications, or the history, involved in it; and, so far as our present knowledge goes, all the details of life in the scenes here illustrated are rendered in accord with the period of the story. To some purely scholastic minds it may seem presumptuous to intermingle translations of notable documents with fanciful illustrations. But, considering the greater precision with which in recent years we have been able to learn the changes and the fashions of ancient life in Egypt, and the essentially unhistorical nature of most of these tales, there seems ample reason to provide such material for the reader's imagination in following the stories; it may-give them more life and reality, and may emphasise the differences which existed between the different periods to which these tales refer. It will be noticed how the growth of the novel is shadowed out in the varied grounds and treatment of the tales. The earliest is purely a collection of marvels or fabulous incidents of the simplest kind. Then we advance to contrasts between town and country, between Egypt and foreign lands. Then personal adventure, and the interest in schemes and successes, becomes the staple material; while only in the later periods does character come in as the groundwork. The same may be seen in English literature--first the tales of wonders and strange lands, then the novel of adventure, and lastly the novel of character. In translating these documents into English I have freely used the various translations already published in other languages; but in all cases more or less revision and retranslation from the original has been made. In this matter I am indebted to Mr. F. Ll. Griffith, who has in some cases--as in Anpu and Bata--almost entirely retranslated the original papyrus. The material followed in each instance will be found stated in the notes accompanying the tales. As to the actual phraseology, I am alone responsible for that. How far original idiom should be retained in any translation is always a debated question, and must entirely depend on the object in view. Here the purpose of rendering the work intelligible to ordinary readers required the modifying of some idioms and the paraphrasing of others. But so far as possible the style and tone of the original has been preserved, and whatever could be easily followed has been left to speak for itself. In many plainnesses of speech the old Egyptian resembled the modern Oriental, or our own forefathers, more than ourselves in this age of squeamishness as yet unparalleled in the world. To avoid offence a few little modifications of words have been made; but rather than give a false impression by tampering with any of the narrative, I have omitted the sequel of the last tale and given only an outline of it. The diction adopted has been the oldest that could be used without affectation when dealing with the early times. It has been purposely modified in the later tales; and in the last --which is of Ptolemaic authorship--a modern style has been followed as more compatible with the later tone of the narrative. For the illustrations Mr. Tristram Ellis's familiarity with Egypt has been of good account in his life-like scenes here used. For each drawing I have searched for the material among the monuments and remains of the age in question. The details of the dresses, the architecture, and the utensils, are all in accord with the period of each tale. In the tale of Setnau two different styles are introduced. Ahura is probably of the time of Amenhotep III., whereas Setnau is a son of Ramessu II.; and the change of fashion between the two different dynasties has been followed as distinctive of the two persons, one a ka or double of the deceased, the other a living man. To the reader who starts with the current idea that all Egyptians were alike, this continual change from one period to another may seem almost fanciful. But it rests on such certain authority that we may hope that this little volume may have its use as an object-lesson in practical archaeology. The use and abuse of notes is a matter of dispute. To be constantly interrupted in reading by some needless and elementary explanation is an impertinence both to the author and the reader: the one cannot resent it, the other therefore resents it for both. But what is to be deemed needless entirely depends on the reader: I have been asked in what country Pompei is, as it is not in the English Gazetteer. Rather than intrude, then, on the reader when he is in high discourse with the ancients, I humbly set up my interpreter's booth

7

next door; and if he cares to call in, and ask about any difficulties, I shall be glad to help him if I can. Not even numbers are intruded to refer to notes; for how often an eager reader has been led off his trail, and turned blithely to refer to 37 or 186 only to find, "See J. Z. xxxviii. 377," at which he gnashed his teeth and cursed such interruptions. So those to whom the original tales are obscure are humbly requested to try for some profit from the remarks after them, that have been gleaned by the translator,

Much might be said by a "folk-lorist"--in proportion to his ardour. But as there are folk-lorists and folk-lorists, and the schools of Rabbi Andrew and Rabbi Joseph write different targums, I have left each to make his own commentary without prejudice.

TALES OF THE MAGICIANS

One day, when King Khufu reigned over all the land, he said to his chancellor, who stood before him, "Go call me my sons and my councillors, that I may ask of them a thing." And his sons and his councillors came and stood before him, and he said to them, "Know ye a man who can tell me tales of the deeds of the magicians?" Then the royal son Khafra stood forth and said, "I will tell thy majesty a tale of the days of thy forefather Nebka, the blessed; of what came to pass when he went into the temple of Ptah of Ankhtaui."

KHAFRA'S TALE

"His majesty was walking unto the temple of Ptah, and went unto the house of the chief reciter Uba-aner, with his train. Now when the wife of Uba-aner saw a page, among those who stood behind the king, her heart longed after him; and she sent her servant unto him, with a present of a box full of garments. "And he came then with the servant. Now there was a lodge in the garden of Uba-aner; and one day the page said to the wife of Uba-aner, 'In the garden of Uba-aner there is now a lodge; behold, let us therein take our pleasure.' So the wife of Uba-aner sent to the steward who had charge over the garden, saying, 'Let the lodge which is in the garden be made ready.' And she remained there, and rested and drank with the page until the sun went down. "And when the even was now come the page went forth to bathe. And the steward said, 'I must go and tell Uba-aner of this matter.' Now when this day was past, and another day came, then went the steward to Uba-aner, and told him of all these things. "Then said Uba-aner, 'Bring me my casket of ebony and electrum.' And they brought it; and he fashioned a crocodile of wax, seven fingers long: and he enchanted it, and said, 'When the page comes and bathes in my lake, seize on him.' And he gave it to the steward, and said to him, 'When the page shall go down into the lake to bathe, as he is daily wont to do, then throw in this crocodile behind him.' And the steward went forth bearing the crocodile. "And the wife of Uba-aner sent to the steward who had charge over the garden, saying, 'Let the lodge which is in the garden be made ready, for I come to tarry there.' "And the lodge was prepared with all good things; and she came and made merry therein with the page. And when the even was now come, the page went forth to bathe as he was wont to do. And the steward cast in the wax crocodile after him into the water; and, behold ! it became a great crocodile seven cubits in length, and it seized on the page. "And Uba-aner abode yet seven days with the king of Upper and Lower Egypt, Nebka, the blessed, while the page was stifled in the crocodile. And after the seven days were passed, the king of Upper and Lower Egypt, Nebka, the blessed, went forth, and Uba-aner went before him. "And Uba-aner said unto his majesty, 'Will your majesty come and see this wonder that has come to pass in your days unto a page?' And the king went with Uba-aner. And Uba-aner called unto the crocodile and said, 'Bring forth the page.' And the crocodile came forth from the Jake with the page. Uba-aner said unto the king, 'Behold, whatever I command this crocodile he will do it.' And his majesty said, 'I pray you send back this crocodile." And Uba-aner stooped and took up the crocodile, and it became in his hand a crocodile of wax. And then Uba-aner told the king that which had passed in his house with the page and his wife. And his majesty said unto the crocodile, 'Take to thee thy prey.' And the crocodile plunged into the lake with his prey, and no man knew whither he went. "And his majesty the king of Upper and Lower Egypt, Nebka, the blessed, commanded, and they brought forth the wife of Uba-aner to the north side of the harem, and burnt her with fire, and cast her ashes in the river "This is a wonder that came to pass in the days of thy forefather the king of Upper and Lower Egypt, Nebka, of the acts of the chief reciter Uba aner." His majesty the king of Upper and Lower Egypt, Khufu, then said, "Let there be presented to the king Nebka, the blessed, a thousand loaves, a hundred draughts of beer, an ox, two jars of incense; and let there be presented a loaf, a jar of beer, a jar of incense, and a piece of meat to the chief reciter Uba-aner; for I have seen the token of his learning." And they did all things as his majesty commanded.

BAUFRA'S TALE

The royal sou Bau-f-ra then stood forth and spake. He said, "I will tell thy majesty of a wonder which came to pass in the days of thy father Seneferu, the blessed, of the deeds of the chief reciter Zazamankh. One day King Seneferu, being weary, went throughout his palace seeking for a pleasure to lighten his heart, but he found none. And he said, 'Haste, and bring before me the chief reciter and scribe of the rolls Zazamankh'; and they straightway brought him. And the king said, 'I have sought in my palace for some delight, but I have found none.' Then said Zazamankh to him, 'Let thy majesty go upon the lake of the palace, and let there be made ready a boat, with all the fair maidens of the harem of thy palace; and the heart of thy majesty shall be refreshed with the sight, in seeing their rowing up and down the water, and seeing the goodly pools of the birds upon the lake, and beholding its sweet fields and grassy shores; thus will thy heart be lightened. And I also will go with thee. Bring me twenty oars of ebony, inlayed with gold, with blades of light wood, inlayed with electrum; and bring me twenty maidens, fair in their limbs, their bosoms and their hair, all virgins; and bring me twenty nets, and give these nets unto the maidens for their garments.' And they did according to all the commands of his majesty. "And they rowed down the stream and up the stream, and the heart of his majesty was glad with the sight of their rowing. But one of them at the steering struck her hair, and her jewel of new malachite fell into the water. And she ceased her song, and rowed not; and her companions ceased, and rowed not. And his majesty said, 'Row you not further?' And they replied, 'Our little steerer here stays and rows not.' His majesty then said to her, 'Wherefore rowest thou not?' She replied, 'It is for my jewel of new malachite which is fallen in the water.' And he said to her, 'Row on, for behold I will replace it.' And she answered, 'But I want my own piece back in its setting.' And his majesty said, 'Haste, bring me the chief reciter Zazamankh,' and they brought him. And his majesty said, Zazamankh, my brother, I have done as thou sayedst, and the heart of his majesty is refreshed with the sight of their rowing. But now a jewel of new malachite of one of the little ones is fallen in the water, and she ceases and rows not, and she has spoilt the rowing of her side. And I said to her, "Wherefore rowest thou not?" and she answered to me, "It is for my jewel of new malachite which is fallen in the water." I replied to her, "Row on, for behold I will replace it"; and she answered to me, "But I want my own piece again back in its setting."' Then the chief reciter Zazamankh spake his magic speech. And he placed one part of the waters of the lake upon the other, and discovered the jewel lying upon a shard; and he took it up and gave it unto its mistress. And the water, which was twelve cubits deep in the middle, reached now to twenty-four cubits after he turned it. And he spake, and used his magic speech; and he brought again the water of the lake to its place. And his majesty spent a joyful day with the whole of the royal house. Then rewarded he the chief reciter Zazamankh with all good things. Behold, this is a wonder that came to pass in the days of thy father, the king of Upper and Lower Egypt, Seneferu, of the deeds of the chief reciter, the scribe of the rolls, Zazamankh." Then said the majesty of the king of Upper and Lower Egypt, Khufu, the blessed, "Let there be presented an offering of a thousand cakes, one hundred draughts of beer, an ox, and two jars of incense to the king of Upper and Lower Egypt, Sene-feru, the blessed; and let there be given a loaf, a jar of beer, and a jar of incense to the chief reciter, the scribe of the rolls, Zazamankh; for I have seen the token of his learning." And they did all things as his majesty commanded.

HORDEDEF'S TALE

THE royal son Hordedef then stood forth and spake. He said, "Hitherto hast thou only heard tokens of those who have gone before, and of which no man knoweth their truth But I will show thy majesty a man of thine own days." And his majesty said, "Who is he, Hordedef?" And the royal son Hordedef answered, "It is a certain man named Dedi, who dwells at Dedsneferu. He is a man of one hundred and ten years old; and he eats five hundred loaves of bread, and a side of beef, and drinks one hundred draughts of beer, unto this day. He knows how to restore the head that is smitten off; he knows how to cause the lion to follow him trailing his halter on the ground; he knows the designs of the dwelling of Tahuti. The majesty of the king of Upper and Lower Egypt, Khufu, the blessed, has long sought for the designs of the dwelling of Tahuti, that he may make the like of them in his pyramid." And his majesty said, "Thou, thyself, Hordedef, my son, bring him to me." Then were the ships made ready for the king's son Hordedef, and he went up the stream to Dedsneferu. And when the ships had moored at the haven, he landed, and sat him in a litter of ebony, the poles of which were of

17

cedar wood overlayed with gold. Now when he drew near to Dedi, they set down the litter. And he arose to greet Dedi, and found him lying on a palmstick couch at the door of his house; one servant held his head and rubbed him, and another rubbed his feet, And the king's son Hordedef said, "Thy state is that of one who lives to good old age; for old age is the end of our voyage, the time of embalming, the time of burial. Lie, then, in the sun, free of infirmities, without the babble of dotage: this is the salutation to worthy age. I come from far to call thee, with a message from my father Khufu, the blessed, for thou shalt eat of the best which the king gives, and of the food which those have who follow after him; that he may bring thee in good estate to thy fathers who are in the tomb." And Dedi replied to him, "Peace to thee! Peace to thee! Hordedef, son of the king, beloved of his father. May thy father Khufu, the blessed, praise thee, may he advance thee amongst the elders, may thy ka prevail against the enemy, may thy soul know the right road to the gate of him who clothes the afflicted; this is the salutation to the king's son." Then the king's son, Hordedef, stretched forth his hands to him, and raised him up, and went with him to the haven, giving unto him his arm. Then said Dedi, "Let there he given me a boat, to bring me my youths and my books." And they made ready for him two boats with their rowers. And Dedi went down the river in the barge in which was the king's son Hordedef. And when he had reached the palace, the king's son, Hordedef, entered in to give account unto his majesty the king of Upper and Lower Egypt, Khufu, the blessed. Then said the king's son Hordedef, "O king, life, wealth, and health! My lord, I have brought Dedi." His majesty replied, "Bring him to me speedily." And his majesty went into the hall of columns of Pharaoh (life, wealth, and health), and Dedi was led before him. And his majesty said, "Wherefore is it, Dedi, that I have not yet seen thee?" And Dedi answered, "He who is called it is that comes; the king (life, wealth, and health) calls me, and behold I come," And his majesty said, "Is it true, that which men say, that thou canst restore the head which is smitten off?" And Dedi replied, "Truly, I know that, O king (life, wealth, and health), my lord." And his majesty said, "Let one bring me a prisoner who is in prison, that his punishment may be fulfilled." And Dedi said, "Let it not be a man, O king, my lord; behold we do not even thus to our cattle." And a duck was brought unto him, and its head was cut off. And the duck was laid on the west side of the hall, and its head on the east side of the hall. And Dedi spake his magic speech. And the duck fluttered along the ground, and its head came likewise; and when it had come part to part the duck stood and quacked. And they brought likewise a goose before him, and he did even so unto it. His majesty caused an ox to be brought, and its head cast on the ground. And Dedi spake his magic speech. And the ox stood upright behind him, and followed him with his halter trailing on the ground. And King Khufu said, "And is it true what is said, that thou knowest the number of the designs of the dwelling of Tahuti?" And Dedi replied, "Pardon me, I know not their number, O king (life, wealth, and health), but I know where they are." And his majesty said, "Where is that?" And Dedi replied, "There is a chest of whetstone in a chamber named the plan-room, in Heli-opolis; they are in this chest." And Dedi said further unto him, "O king (life, wealth, and health), my lord, it is no It that is to bring them to thee." And his m'jesty said, "Who, then, is it that shall bring them to me?" And Dedi answered to him, "It is the eldest of the three children who are in the body of

Rud-didet who shall bring them to thee." And his majesty said, "Would that it may be as thou sayest! And who is this Rud-didet?" And Dedi replied, "She is the wife of a priest of Ra, lord of Sakhebu. And she has conceived these three sons by Ra, lord of Sakhebu, and the god has promised her that they shall fulfil this noble office (of reigning) over all this land, and that the eldest of them shall be high priest in Heliopolis." And his majesty's heart became troubled for this; but Dedi spake unto him, "What is this that thou thinkest, O king (life, wealth, health), my lord? Is it because of these three children? I tell thee thy son shall reign, and thy son's son, and then one of them." His majesty said, "And when shall Rud-didet bear these? "And he replied, "She shall bear them on the 26th of the month Tybi." And his majesty said, "When the banks of the canal of Letopolis are cut, I will walk there that I may see the temple of Ra, lord of Sakhebu." And Dedi replied, "Then I will cause that there be four cubits of water by the banks ot the canal of Letopolis." When his majesty returned to his palace, his majesty said, "Let them place Dedi in the house of the royal son Hordedef, that he may dwell with him, and let them give him a daily portion of a thousand loaves, a hundred draughts of beer, an ox, and a hundred bunches of onions." And they did everything as his majesty commanded. And one day it came to pass that Rud-didet felt the pains of birth. And the majesty of Ra, lord of Sakhebu, said unto Isis, to Nebhat, to Meskhent, to Hakt, and to Khnumu, "Go ye, and deliver Rud-didet of these three children that she shall bear, who are to fulfil this noble office over all this land; that they may build up your temples, furnish your altars with offerings, supply your tables of libation, and increase your endowments." Then went these deities; their fashion they made as that of dancing girls, and Khnumu was with them as a porter. They drew near unto the house of Ra-user, and found him standing, with his girdle fallen. And they played before him with their instruments of music. But he said unto them, "My ladies, behold, here is a woman who feels the pains of birth." They said to him, "Let us see her, for we know how to help her." And he replied, "Come, then." And they entered in straightway to Rud-didet, and they closed the door on her and on themselves. Then Isis stood before her, and Nebhat stood behind her, and Hakt helped her. And Isis said, "O child, by thy name of User-ref, do not do violence." And the child came upon her hands, as a child of a cubit; its bones were strong, the beauty of its limbs was like gold, and its hair was like true lapis lazuli. They washed him, and prepared him, and placed him on a carpet on the brickwork. Then Meskhent approached him and said, "This is a king who shall reign over all the land." And Khnumu gave strength to his limbs. Then Isis stood before her, and Nebhat stood behind her, and Hakt helped her. And Isis said, "O child, by thy name of Sah-ra, stay not in her." Then the child came upon her hands, a child of a cubit; its bones were strong, the beauty of its limbs was like gold, and its hair was like true lapis lazuli. They washed him, and prepared him, and layed him on a carpet on the brickwork. Then Meskhent approached him and said, "This is a king who shall reign over all the land." And Khnumu gave strength to his limbs. Then Isis stood before her, and Nebhat stood behind her, and Hakt helped her. And Isis said, "O child, by thy name of Kaku, remain not in darkness in her." And the child came upon her hands, a child of a cubit; its bones were strong, the beauty of its limbs was like gold, and its hair was like true lapis lazuli. And Meskhent approached him and said, "This is a king who shall reign over all the land." And Khnumu gave strength to his limbs. And they washed him, and prepared him, and layed him on a carpet on the brickwork. And the deities went out, having delivered Rud-didet of the three children. And they said, "Rejoice! O Ra-user, for behold three children are born unto thee." And he said unto them, "My ladies, and what shall I give unto ye? Behold, give this bushel of barley here unto your porter, that ye may take it as your reward to the brew-house." And Khnumu loaded himself with the bushel of barley. And they went away toward the place from which they came. And Isis spake unto these goddesses, and said, "Wherefore have we come without doing a marvel for these children, that we may tell it to their father who has sent us?" Then made they the divine diadems of the king (life, wealth, and health), and laid them in the bushel of barley. And they caused the clouds to come with wind and rain; and they turned back again unto the house. And they said, "Let us put this barley in a closed chamber, sealed up, until we return northward, dancing." And they placed the barley in a close chamber. And Rud-didet purified herself, with a purification of fourteen days. And she said to her handmaid, "Is the house made ready?" And she replied, "All things are made ready, but the brewing barley is not yet brought." And Rud-didet said, "Wherefore is the brewing barley not yet brought? " And the servant answered, " It would all of it long since be ready if the barley had not been given to the dancing-girls, and lay in the chamber under their seal." Rud didet said, "Go down, and bring of it, and Ra-user shall give them in its stead when he shall come," And the handmaid went, and opened the chamber. And she heard talking and singing, music and dancing, quavering, and all things which are performed for a king in his chamber. And she returned and told to Rud-didet all that she had heard. And she went through the chamber, but she found not the place where the sound was. And she layed her temple to the sack, and found that the sounds were in it. She placed it in a chest, and put that in another locker, and tied it fast with leather, and layed it in the store-room, where the things were, and sealed it. And Ra-user came returning from the field; and Rud-didet repeated unto him these things; and his heart was glad above all things; and they sat down and made a joyful day. And after these days it came to pass that Rud-didet was wroth with her servant, and beat her with stripes. And the servant said unto those that were in the house, "Shall it be done thus unto me? She has borne three kings, and I will go and tell this to his majesty King Khufu the blessed." And she went, and found the eldest brother of her mother, who was binding his flax on the floor. And he said to her, "Whither goest thou, my little maid?" And she told him of all these things. And her brother said to her, "Wherefore comest thou thus to me? Shall I agree to treachery? " And he took a bunch of the flax to her, and laid on her a violent blow. And the servant went to fetch a handful of water, and a crocodile carried her away. Her uncle went therefore to tell of this to Rud-didet; and he found Rud-didet sitting, her head on her knees, and her heart beyond measure sad. And he said to her, "My lady, why makest thou thy heart thus?" And she answered, "It is because of this little wretch that was in the house; behold she went out saying, 'I will go and tell it.'" And he bowed his head unto the ground, and said, "My lady, she came and told me of these things, and made her complaint unto me; and I laid on her a violent blow. And she went forth to draw water, and a crocodile carried her away." (The rest of the tale is lost.]

REMARKS

The tales or the magicians are only preserved in a single copy, and of that the beginning is entirely lost. The papyrus was brought from Egypt by an English traveller, and was purchased by the Berlin Museum from the property of Lepsius, who had received it from the owner, Miss Westcar: hence it is known as the Westcar papyrus. It was written probably in the XIIth Dynasty, but -doubtless embodied tales, which had been floating for generations before, about the names of the early kings. It shows us probably the kind of material that existed for the great recension of the pre-monu-mental history, made in the time of Seti I. Those ages of the first three dynasties were as long before that recension as we are after it; and this must always be remembered in considering the authority of the Egyptian records. This papyrus has been more thoroughly studied than most, perhaps more than any other. Erman has devoted two volumes to it; publishing the whole in photographic facsimile, transcribed in hieroglyphs, transcribed in the modern alphabet, translated literally, translated freely, commented on and discussed word by word, and with a complete glossary of all words used in it. This exhaustive publication is named "Der Marchen des Papyrus Westcar." Moreover, Maspero has given a current translation in the "Contes Populaires," 2nd edit. pp. 53-86. The scheme of these tales is that they are all told to King Khufu by his sons; and as the beginning is lost, eight lines are here added to explain this and introduce the subject. The actual papyrus begins with the last few words of a previous tale concerning some other magician under an earlier king. Then comes the tale of Khafra, next that of Bau-f-ra, and lastly that of Hor-dedef.

It need hardly be said that these tales are quite fictitious. The king and his successor Khafra are real, but the other sons cannot be identified; and the confusion of supposing three kings of the Vth Dynasty to be triplets born early in the IVth Dynasty, shows what very vague ideas of their own history the Egyptians had when these tales were formed. This does not prevent our seeing that they embodied some very important traditions, and gives us an unequalled picture of the early civilisation. In the earliest tale or the three there seems at first sight merely a sketch of faithlessness and revenge. But there is probably much more in it. To read it aright we must bear in mind the position of woman in ancient Egypt. If, in later ages, Islam has gone to the extreme of the man determining his own divorce at a word, in early times almost the opposite system prevailed. All property belonged to the woman; all that a man could earn, or inherit, was made over to his wife; and families always reckoned back further on the mother's side than the father's. As the changes in historical times have been in the direction of men's rights, it is very unlikely that this system of female predominance was invented or introduced, but rather that it descends from primitive times. In this tale we see, then, at the beginning of our knowledge of the country, the clashing of two different social systems. The reciter is strong for men's rights, he brings destruction on the wife, and never even gives her name, but always calls her merely "the wife of Uba-aner." But behind all this there is probably the remains of a very different system. The servant employed by the mistress seems to see nothing outrageous in her proceedings; and even the steward, who is on the master's side, waits a day or two before reporting matters. When we remember the supremacy in properly and descent which women held in Egypt, and then read this tale, it seems that it belongs to the close of a social system like that of the Nairs, in which the lady makes her selection--with variations from time to time. The incident of sending a present of clothing is curiously like the tale about a certain English envoy, whose proprieties were sadly ruffled in the Nair country, when a lady sent him a grand shawl with an intimation of her choice. The priestesses of Amen retained to the last this privilege of choice, as being under divine, and not human protection; but it seems to have become unseemly in late times. The hinging of this tale, and of those that follow it, upon the use of magic, shows how thoroughly the belief in magic powers was ingrained in the Egyptians. Now such a belief implies the presence of magicians, and shows how familiar must have been the claim to such powers, and the practising of the tricks of witchcraft, so prevalent in Africa in modern times. The efficacy of a model, such as this crocodile of wax, is an idea continually met with in Egypt. The system of tomb furniture and decoration, of ka statues, of ushabtis or figures to work for the deceased, and the models placed in foundation deposits, all show how a model was supposed to have the efficacy of an actual reality. Even in the latest tale of all (written in Ptolemaic times), Setnau makes a model of a boat and men, to be sunk in the river to work for him. The reconversion of the crocodile to wax, on being taken up by the magician, reminds us of the serpent becoming again a rod when taken up by Aaron. The punishment of burning alive is very rarely, if ever, mentioned in Egyptian history, though it occurs in modern Egyptian tales: and it looks as if it were brought in here rather as a dire horror for the climax than as a probable incident. The place of the penalty, in front of the harem, or the private portion of the palace, was evidently for the intimi-' dation of other ladies. At the close of each tale, King Khufu, to whom it is told, orders funerary offerings by the usual formula, to be presented in honour of the king under whom the wonder took place. On the tablets of the tombs in the early times, there is usually recorded the offering--or, rather, the pious desire that there should be offered--thousands of loaves, of oxen, of gazelles, of cranes, &c., for a deceased person. Such expression cost no more by the thousand than by the dozen, so thousands came to be the usual expression in all ordaining of offerings.

We are so accustomed to think of tedium as something modern, that it seems strange to find in the oldest tales in the world how the first

31

king of whom we know anything was bored by his pleasures. A reward for discovering a new pleasure is the very basis of the tale of Sneferu; and the wise man's remedy of a day in the country is still the best resource, though all that we know as human history has tried its experiments in enjoyment since then. The flavour of the ballet thrown in, by the introduction of the damsels of the household clad in fishing nets, is not yet obsolete in modern amusements; and even in this century Muhammed Ali had resource to the same way of killing time, as he was rowed about by his harem, but on an artificial lake. The use of two large oars for steering explains the detail of the story. The oars were one on each side of the stern, and were each managed by a steerer. From the tale we see that the steerer led the song of the rowers, and if the leader ceased, all that side of the boat ceased also.. The position of the lost jewel upon the hair shows that it was in a fillet set with inlaying, like that seen on early figures, such as Nefert at Medum, who wears a fillet of rosettes to retain the hair; and the position of the steering oar attached to a post, with the handle rising high in the air, explains how it could strike the fillet and displace the jewel. The last tale is really double, a tale within a tale. It begins with the wonders done by Dedi, and then goes on with the history or the children about whom he prophesied to Khufu. The village of Dedi was probably near Medum, as in the temple of Sneferu at Medum an offering was found presented by a worshipper to the gods of Ded-sneferu: hence the background which is here given for the scene of Hordedef leading old Dedi. The translation of "the designs of the dwelling of Tahuti" is not certain; but the passage seems to refer to some architectural plan which was desired for the pyramid. The story of Rud-didet is remarkable historically. She is said to be wife of the priest of Ra, her children are sons of Ra, and they are the first three kings of the Vth dynasty, and supplanted the line of Khufu. This points to the Vth Dynasty having been a priestly usurpation; and on looking at its history we see two confirmations of this. The title "Son of Ra" is so common in most ages in Egypt that it is taken for granted, and is applied in lists to any second cartouche; but it is not found until well into the Vth Dynasty; the earlier kings were not descendants of Ra, and it is only on arriving at this dynasty, which claimed descent from Ra, through the wife of the priest of Ra, that we find the claim of each king to be a "son of Ra."

Another confirmation of this priestly descent is the abundance of priesthoods established for the kings of the Vth Dynasty; a care which agrees with their having a priestly origin; while in the tale it is particularly said that they would build up the temples, furnish the altars with offerings, supply the tables of libations, and increase the religious endowments. The names of the three children are a play upon the names of the first three kings of the Vth Dynasty. User-kaf is made into User-ref; Sahu-ra is written Sah-ra; and Kaka is Kaku; thus making allusions to their births. The comparison of the hair to true lapis lazuli seems very strange; but there is often a confusion between black aind blue in uneducated races, and azrak means either dark blue or green, or black, at present in Arabic. Lapis lazuli is brought in to the name of the queen of Ramessu who was called "gold and lazuli," Nub-khesdeb; recalling the comparison here of personal beauty to these precious materials. It is noticeable here that in a tale of the Vth Dynasty, certainly written as early as the XIIth Dynasty, we find professional dancers commonly recognised, and going on travels through the country, with a porter. From this tale we also learn that Egyptian women underwent a purification of fourteen days, during which they kept apart and did not attend to any household matters. The mistress of the house here inquires if the preparations are made for the feast on her return to household affairs; and hears then how the beer cannot be made for lack of the barley. The securing of the sack is just in accord with the remains of this early period; the use of boxes, of thongs of leather for tying and of clay sealings for securing property, were all familiar matters in the XIIth Dynasty, as we learn from Kahun.

The present close of the tale is evidently only a stage in it, when the treacherous maid meets with the common doom of the wicked in Egyptian romance. How it was continued is a matter of speculation, but Khufu ought certainly to reappear and to order great rewards for Dedi, who up to this has only had maintenance on his requisite scale provided for him. Yet it is imperative that the children shall be saved from his wrath, as they are the kings of the Vth Dynasty. There may be a long episode lost of their flight and adventures. One reference to a date needs notice. The 25th of the month Tybi is said to be the predicted birthday of the children; and Khufu refers to going to Sakhebu about that time apparently, when the banks of the canal are cut and the land was drying after the inundation, whereon Dedi threatens that the water shall still be deep there. This points to 25th Tybi being about the close of the inundation. This would be about the case both in the beginning of the IVth Dynasty, and also in the XIIth Dynasty, when the papyrus was perhaps written: hence there is nothing conclusive to be drawn from this allusion so far. But when we compare this tale with those following, we see good ground for its belonging to a time before the XIIth Dynasty The following tale of the peasant and the workman evidently belongs to the IXth or Xth Dynasties, when Herakleopolis was the capital, and Sanehat is certainly of the XIIth Dynasty. Yet in those we see character and incident made the basis of interest, in place of the childish profusion of marvels of the Tales of the Magicians. It seems impossible not to suppose that they belong to very different ages and canons of taste; and hence we cannot refer the crudities ot the Khufu tales to the time of the far more elaborate and polished recital of the adventures of Sanehat in the XIIth Dynasty. Being thus obliged to suppose an earlier date for these tales, the allusion to the month Tybi throws us back to a very early period--the IVth Dynasty --for their original outlines. Doubtless they were modified by reciters, and probably took shape in the Vth or VIth Dynasties; but yet we must regard them as belonging practically to the age to which they refer.

IXTH DYNASTY

THE PEASANT AND THE WORKMAN

There dwelt in the Sekhet Hemat--or salt country--a peasant called the Sekhti, with his wife and children, his asses and his dogs; and he trafficked in all good things of the Sekhet Hemat to Henenseten. Behold now he went with rushes, natron, and salt, with wood and pods, with stones and seeds, and all good products of the Sekhet Hemat. And this Sekhti journeyed to the south unto Henenseten; and when he came to the lands of the house of Fefa, north of Denat, he found a man there standing on the bank, a man called Hemti--the workman--son of a man called Asri, who was a serf of the High Steward Meruitensa. Now said this Hemti, when he saw the asses of Sekhti, that were pleasing in his eyes, "Oh that some good god would grant me to steal away the goods of Sekhti from him!" Now the Hemti's house was by the dyke of the tow-path, which was straitened, and not wide, as much as the width of a waist cloth: on the one side of it was the water, and on the other side of it grew his corn. Hemti said then to his servant, "Hasten I bring me a shawl from the house," and it was brought instantly. Then spread he out this shawl on the face of the dyke, and it lay with its fastening on the water and its fringe on the corn. Now Sekhti approached along the path used by all men. Said Hemti, "Have a care, Sekhti! you are not going to trample on my clothes! "Said Sekhti, "I will do as you like, I will pass carefully." Then went he up on the higher side. But Hemti said, "Go you over my corn, instead of the path?" Said Sekhti, "I am going carefully; this high field of corn is not my choice, but you have stopped your path with your clothes, and will you then not let us pass by the side of the path?" And one of the asses filled its mouth with a cluster of corn. Said Hemti, "Look you, I shall take away your ass, Sekhti, for eating my corn; behold it will have to pay according to the amount of the injury." Said Sekhti, "I am going carefully; the one way is stopped, therefore took I my ass by the enclosed ground, and do you seize it for filling its mouth with a cluster of corn? Moreover, I know unto whom this domain belongs, even unto the Lord Steward Meruitensa. He it is who smites every robber in this whole land; and shall I then be robbed in his domain?" Said Hemti, "This is the proverb which men speak: 'A poor man's name is only his own matter.' I am he of whom you spake, even the Lord Steward of whom you think." Thereon he took to him branches of green tamarisk and scourged all his limbs, took his asses, and drave them into the pasture. And Sekhti wept very greatly, by reason of the pain of what he had suffered. Said Hemti, "Lift not up your voice, Sekhti, or you shall go to the Demon of Silence." Sekhti answered, "You beat me, you steal my goods, and now would take away even my voice, O demon of silence! If you will restore my goods, then will I cease to cry out at your violence." Sekhti stayed the whole day petitioning Hemti, but he would not give ear unto him. And Sekhti went his way to Khenensuten to complain to the Lord Steward Meruitensa. He found him coming out from the door of his house to embark on his boat, that he might go to the judgment hall. Sekhti said, "Ho! turn, that I may please thy heart with this discourse. Now at this time let one of thy followers whom thou wilt, come to me that I may send him to thee concerning it." The Lord Steward Meruitensa made his follower, whom he chose, go straight unto him, and Sekhti sent him back with an account of all these matters. Then the Lord Steward

Meruitensa accused Hemti unto the nobles who sat with him; and they said unto him, "By your leave: As to this Sekhti of yours, let him bring a witness. Behold thou it is our custom with our Sekhtis; witnesses come with them; behold, that is our custom. Then it will be fitting to beat this Hemti for a trifle of natron and a trifle of salt; if he is commanded to pay for it, he will pay for it." But the High Steward Meruitensa held his peace; for he would not reply unto these nobles, but would reply unto the Sekhti. Now Sekhti came to appeal to the Lord Steward Meruitensa, and said, " O my Lord Steward, greatest of the great, guide of the needy: When thou embarkest on the lake of truth,-- Mayest thou sail upon it with a fair wind; May thy mainsail not fly loose. May there not be lamentation in thy cabin; May not misfortune come after thee. May not thy mainstays be snapped; Mayest thou not run aground. May not the wave seize thee; Mayest thou not taste the impurities of the river; Mayest thou not see the face of fear. May the fish come to thee without escape; Mayest thou reach unto plump waterfowl.

For thou art the orphan's father, the widow's husband, The desolate woman's brother, the garment of the motherless. Let me celebrate thy name in this land for every virtue. A guide without greediness of heart; A great one without any meanness. Destroying deceit, encouraging justice; Coming to the cry, and allowing utterance. Let me speak, do thou hear and do justice; O praised! whom the praised ones praise. Abolish oppression, behold me, I am overladen, Reckon with me, behold me defrauded." Now the Sekhti made this speech in the time of the majesty of the King Neb-ka-n-ra, blessed. The Lord Steward Meruitensa went away straight to the king and said, "My lord, I have found one of these Sekhti, excellent of speech, in very truth; stolen are his goods, and he has come to complain to me of the matter." His majesty said, "As thou wishest that I may see health! lengthen out his complaint, without replying to any of his speeches. He who desireth him to continue speaking should be silent; behold, bring us his words in writing, that we may listen to them. But provide for his wife and his children, and let the Sekhti himself also have a living. Thou must cause one to give him his portion without letting him know that thou art he who is giving it to him." There were given to him four loaves and two draughts of beer each day; which the Lord Steward Meruitensa provided for him, giving it to a friend of his, who furnished it unto him. Then the Lord Steward Meruitensa sent the governor of the Sekhet Hemat to make provision for the wife of the Sekhti, three rations of corn each day. Then came the Sskhti a second time, and even a third time, unto the Lord Steward Meruitensa; but he told two of his followers to go unto the Sekhti, and seize on him, and beat him with staves. But he came again unto him, even unto six times, and said, "My Lord Steward-Destroying deceit, and encouraging justice; Raising up every good thing, and crushing every evil; As plenty comes removing famine, As clothing covers nakedness, As clear sky after storm warms the shivering; As fire cooks that which is raw, As water quenches the thirst; Look with thy face upon my lot; do not covet, but content me without fail; do the right and do not evil." But yet Meruitensa would not hearken unto his complaint; and the Sekhti came yet, and yet again, even unto the ninth time. Then the Lord Steward told two of his followers to go unto the Sekhti; and the Sekhti feared that he should be beaten as at the third request. But the Lord Steward Meruitensa then sa;d unto him, "Fear not, Sekhti, for what thou has done. The Sekhti has made many speeches, delightful to the heart of his majesty and I take an oath--as I eat bread, and as I drink water--that thou shalt be remembered to eternity." Said the Lord Steward, "Moreover, thou shalt be satisfied when thou shalt hear of thy complaints" He caused to be written on a clean roll of papyrus each petition to the end, and the Lord Steward Meruitensa sent it to the majesty of the King Neb-ka-n-ra, blessed, and it was good to him more than anything that is in the whole land: but his majesty said to Meruitensa, "Judge it thyself; I do not desire it." The Lord Steward Meruitensa made two of his followers to go to the Sekhet Hemat, and bring a list of the household of the Sekhti; and its amount was six persons, beside his oxen and his goats, his wheat and his barley, his asses and his dogs; and moreover he gave all that which belonged unto the Hemti to the Sekhti, even all his property and his offices, and the Sekhti was beloved of the king more than all his overseers, and ate of all the good things of the king, with all his household.

Of the tale of the peasant and the workman three copies, more or less imperfect, remain to us. At Berlin are two papyri, Nos. 2 and 4, containing parts of the tale, published in fascimile in the "Denkmaler" of Lepsius vi. 108-110 and 113; while portions of another copy exist in the Butler papyrus; and lately fragments of the same have been collated in the collection of Lord Amherst of Hackney. These last have been published in the Proceedings of the Society of Biblical Archaeology, xiv. 558. The number of copies seem to show that this was a popular tale in early times; it certainly is of a more advanced type than the earlier tales of magic, though it belongs to a simpler style than the tales which follow. It has been translated partially by Chabas and Goodwin, and also by Maspero, but most completely by Griffith in the Proceedings of the Society of Biblical Archaeology, referred to above.

The beginning of the tale is lost in all the copies, and an introductory sentence is here added in brackets, to explain the position of affairs at the opening of the fragment. The essence of the tale is the difference in social position between the Sekhti, or peasant, and the Hemti, or workman--the fellah and the client of the noble; and the impossibility of getting justice against a client, unless by some extraordinary means of attracting his patron's attention, is the basis of the action. There is not a single point of incident here which might not be true in modern times; every turn of it seems to live, as one reads it in view of country life in Egypt. The region of the tale is Henenseten, or Herakleopolis, now Ahnas, a little south of the Fayum. This was the seat of the IXth and Xth Dynasties, apparently ejected from Memphis by a foreign invasion of the Delta; and here it is that the High Steward lives and goes to speak to the king. The district of the Sekhti is indicated by his travelling south to Henenseten, and going with asses and not by boat. Hence we are led to look for the Sekhet Hemat, or salt country, in the borders of the Fayum lake, whence the journey would be southward, and across the desert. This lake was not regulated artificially until the XIIth Dynasty; and hence at the period of this tale it was a large sheet of water, fluctuating with each rise and fall of the Nile, and bordered by lagoons where rushes would flourish, and where salt and natron would accumulate daring the dry season of each year. At the present time the lake of the Fayum is brackish, and the cliffs which border it contain so much salt that rain pools which collect on them are not drinkable. The paths and roads of Egypt are not protected by law as in Western countries. Each person encroaches on a path or diverts it as may suit his purpose, only checked by the liberties taken by passers-by in trespassing if a path be insufficient. Hence, it is very usual to see a house built over half of a path, and driving the traffic into the field or almost over the river bank. In this case the Hemti had taken in as much of the path as he could, and left it but a narrow strip along the top of the canal bank. The frequent use of the public way for drying clothes, or spreading out property, gave the idea of choking the way altogether, and leaving no choice but trespassing on the crops. No sooner does a donkey pause, or even pass, by a field of corn than he snatches a mouthful, and in a delay or altercation such as this the beast is sure to take the advantage. Donkeys carrying loads by cornfields are usually muzzled with rope nets, to prevent their feeding; and even sheep and goats are also fended in the same way. The proverb, "A poor man's name is only his own matter," refers to the independent fellah having no patron or protector who will take up and defend his name from accusations, as the interests of clients and serfs would be protected. This being the case, Hemti therefore seizes on the property, and drives the asses into his own pasture field. The scene of Meruitensa laying the case before the nobles who sat with him is interesting as showing that even simple cases were not decided by one judge, but referred to a council. Similarly, Una lays stress on the private trial of the queen being confided to him and only one other judge. Apparently, referring cases to a bench of judges was the means of preventing corruption. The speeches of the Sekhti were given at full length in the papyrus, but owing to injuries we cannot now entirely recover them; they are all in much the same strain, only the first and last are translated here, and the others are passed over. The style of these speeches was evidently looked on as eloquent in those days, and this papyrus really seems to show the time when long-drawn comparisons and flowery wishes were in fashion. It is far different from later compositions, as it is also from the earlier simple narration of crude marvels in the tales of the magicians. The close of the tale is defective, but from the remains it appears to have ended by the gift of the Hemti's property to the oppressed Sekhti and the triumph of the injured peasant.

XIITH DYNASTY

THE SHIPWRECKED SAILOR

The wise servant said, " Let thy heart be satisfied, O my lord, for that we have come back to the country; after we have long been on board, and rowed much, the prow has at last touched land. All the people rejoice, and embrace us one after another. Moreover, we have come back in good health, and not a man is lacking; although we have been to the ends of Wawat, and gone through the land of Senmut, we have returned in peace, and our land--behold, we have come back to it. Hear me, my lord; I have no other refuge. Wash thee, and turn the water over thy ringers; then go and tell the tale to the majesty." His lord replied, "Thy heart continues still its wandering words! but although the mouth of a man may save him, his words may also cover his face with confusion. Wilt thou do then as thy heart moves thee? This that thou wilt say, tell quietly " The sailor then answered, "Now I shall tell that which has happened to me, to my very self I was going to the mines of Pharaoh, and I went down on the sea on a ship of 150 cubits long and 40 cubits wide, with 150 sailors of the best of Egypt, who had seen heaven and earth, and whose hearts were stronger than lions. They had said that the wind would not be contrary, or that there would be none. But as we approached the land the wind arose, and threw up waves eight cubits high. As for me, I seized a piece of wood; but those who were in the vessel perished, without one remaining. A wave threw me on an island, after that I had been three days alone, without a companion beside my own heart. I laid me in a thicket, and the shadow covered me. Then stretched I my limbs to try to find something for my mouth. I found there figs and grapes, all manner of good herbs, berries and grain, melons of all kinds, fishes and birds. Nothing was lacking. And I satisfied myself; and left on the ground that which was over, of what my arms had been filled withal. I dug a pit, I lighted a fire, and I made a burntoffering unto the gods. "Suddenly I heard a noise as of thunder, which I thought to be that of a wave of the sea. The trees shook, and the earth was moved. I uncovered my face, and I saw that a serpent drew near. He was thirty cubits long, and his beard greater than two cubits; his body was as overlayed with gold, and his colour as that of true lazuli. He coiled himself before me. "Then he opened his mouth, while that I lay on my face before him, and he said to me, 'What has brought thee, what has brought thee, little one, what has brought thee? If thou sayest not speedily what has brought thee to this isle, I will make thee know thyself; as a flame thou shalt vanish, if thou tellest me not something I have not heard, or which I knew not, before thee.' "Then he took me in his mouth and carried me to his resting-place, and layed me down without any hurt. I was whole and sound, and nothing was gone from me. Then he opened his mouth against me, while that I lay on my face before him, and he said, 'What has brought thee, what has brought thee, little one, what has brought thee to this isle which is in the sea, and of which the shores are in the midst of the waves?' "Then I replied to him, and holding my arms low before him, I said to him, 'I was embarked for the mines by the order of the majesty, in a ship, 150 cubits was its length, and the width of it 40 cubits. It had 150 sailors of the best of Egypt, who had seen heaven and earth, and the hearts of whom were stronger than lions. They said that the wind would not be contrary, or that there would be none. Each of them exceeded his companion in the prudence of his heart and the strength of his arm, and I was not beneath any of them. A storm came upon us while we were on the sea. Hardly could we reach to the shore when the wind waxed yet greater, and the waves rose even eight cubits. As for me, I seized a piece of wood, while those who were in the boat perished without one being left with me for three days. Behold me now before thee, for I was brought to this isle by a wave of the sea.' "Then said he to me, 'Fear not, fear not, little one, and make not thy face sad. If thou hast come to me, it is God who has let thee live. For it is He who has brought thee to this isle of the blest, where nothing is lacking, and which is filled with all good things. See now, thou shalt pass one month after another, until thou shalt be four months in this isle. Then a ship shall come from thy land with sailors, and thou shalt leave with them and go to thy country, and thou shalt die in thy town. '"Converse is pleasing, and he who tastes of it passes over his misery.

I will therefore tell thee of that which is in this isle. I am here with my brethren and my children around me; we are seventy-five serpents, children, and kindred; without naming a young girl who was brought unto me by chance, and on whom the fire of heaven fell, and burnt her to ashes. "'As for thee if thou art strong, and if thy heart waits patiently, thou shalt press thy infants to thy bosom and embrace thy wife. Thou shalt return to thy house which is full of all good things, thou shalt see thy land, where thou shalt dwell in the midst of thy kindred.' "Then I bowed, in my obeisance, and I touched the ground before him. 'Behold now that which I have told thee before. I shall tell of thy presence unto Pharaoh, I shall make him to know of thy greatness, and I will bring to thee of the sacred oils and perfumes, and of incense of the temples with which all gods are honoured. I shall tell, moreover, of that which I do now see (thanks to him), and there shall be rendered to thee praises before the fulness of all the land. I shall slay asses for thee in sacrifice, I shall pluck for thee the birds, and I shall bring for thee ships full of all kinds of the treasures of Egypt, as is comely to do unto a god, a friend of men in a far country, of which men know not.' "Then he smiled at my speech, because of that which was in his heart, for he said to me, 'Thou art not rich in perfumes, for all that thou hast is but common incense. As for me I am prince of the land of Punt, and I have perfumes. Only the oil which thou sayedst thou wouldest bring is not common in this isle. But, when thou shalt depart from this place, thou shalt never more see this isle; it shall be changed into waves.' "And, behold, when the ship drew near, according to all that he had told me before, I got me up into an high tree, to strive to see those who were within it. Then I came and told to him this matter; but it was already known unto him before. Then he said to me. 'Farewell, farewell, go to thy house, little one, see again thy children, and let thy name be good in thy town; these are my wishes for thee.' "Then I bowed myself before him, and held my arms low before him, and he, he gave me gifts of precious perfumes, of cassia, of sweet woods, of kohl, of cypress, an abundance of incense, of ivory tusks, of baboons, of apes, and all kind of precious things. I embarked all in the ship which was come, and bowing myself, I prayed God for him. "Then he said to me, 'Behold thou shalt come to thy country in two months, thou shalt press to thy bosom thy children, and thou shalt rest in thy tomb.' After this I went down to the shore unto the ship, and I called to the sailors who were there. Then on the shore I rendered adoration to the master of this isle and to those who dwelt therein. "When we shall come, in our return, to the house of Pharaoh, in the second month, according to all that the serpent has said, we shall approach unto the palace. And I shall go in before Pharaoh, I shall bring the gifts which I have brought from this isle into the country. Then he shall thank me before the fulness of all the land. Grant then unto me a follower, and lead me to the courtiers of the king. Cast thy eye upon me, after that I am come to land again, after that I have both seen and proved this. Hear my prayer, for it is good to listen to people. It was said unto me, 'Become a wise man, and thou shalt come to honour,' and behold I have become such." This is finished from its beginning unto its end, even as it was found in a writing. It is written by the scribe of cunning fingers Ameni-amen-aa; may he live in life, wealth, and health! REMARKS This tale is only known in one copy, preserved in the Hermitage collection at St. Petersburg. The papyrus has not yet been published, either in facsimile or transcription. But two translations of it have appeared by M. Golenischeff: from the earlier a modified translation is given by Maspero in the "Contes Populaires," 2nd edit., pp. 133-146, and the later translation is in M. Golenischeff's excellent

"Inventaire de la collection Egyptienne (Ermitage Imperial)," p. 177-182. The tale is that of a returned sailor, speaking to his superior and telling his adventures, to induce him to send him on with an introduction to the king. At first his master professes to disbelieve him, and then the sailor protests that this happened to himself, and gives his narrative. The idea of an enchanted island, which has risen from the waves and will sink again, is here found to be one of the oldest plots for a tale of marvels. But the construction is far more advanced than that of the tales of the magicians. The family of serpents and the manner of the great serpent is well conceived, and there are many fine touches of literary quality: such as noise as of thunder, the trees shaking and the earth being moved at the appearance of the great serpent--the speeches of the serpent and his threat--the sailors who had seen heaven and earth--the contempt of the serpent for his offerings, "As for me, I am prince of the land of Punt, and I have perfumes"--and the scene of departure. All of these points show a firm hand and practised taste, although there is still a style of simplicity clinging to it which agrees well to its date in the XIIth Dynasty. The great serpent is not of a type usual in Egyptian designs. The human-headed uraeus is seldom bearded; and the best example of such a monster is on an Ethiopian temple, where a great uraeus has human arms and a lion's head. The colours again repeat the favourite combination expressive of splendour--gold and lazuli. Though lazuli is very rare in early times, yet it certainly was known in the XIIth Dynasty, as shown by the forms of some beads of lazuli. The slaughter of asses in sacrifice is a very peculiar offering, and no sign of this is found in any representations or groups of offerings.

The colophon of the copyist at the end shows by the style of the name that it belongs to the earlier part of the XIIth Dynasty, and if so, the composition might be referred to the opening of foreign trade under Sankhkara or Amenemhat I.

XIITH DYNASTY

THE ADVENTURES OF SANEHAT

The hereditary prince, royal seal-bearer, confidential friend, judge, keeper of the gate of the foreigners, true and beloved royal acquaintance, the royal follower Sanehat says:-- I attended my lord as a follower of the king, of the house of the hereditary princess, the greatly favoured, the royal wife, Ankhet-Usertesen, who shares the dwelling of the royal son Amenemhat in Kanefer. In the thirtieth year, the month Paophi, the seventh day the god entered his horizon, the king Sehotepabra flew up to heaven and joined the sun's disc, the follower of the god met his maker. The palace was silenced, and in mourning, the great gates were closed, the courtiers crouching on the ground, the people in hushed mourning. His majesty had sent a great army with the nobles to the land of the Temehu (Lybia), his son and heir, the good god king Usertesen as their leader. Now he was returning, and had brought away living captives and all kinds of cattle without end. The councillors of the palace had sent to the West to let the king know the matter that had come to pass in the inner hall. The messenger was to meet him on the road, and reach him at the time of evening: the matter was urgent. "A hawk had soared with his followers." Thus said he, not to let the army know of it Even if the royal sons who commanded in that army send a message, he was not to speak to a single one of them. But I was standing near, and heard his voice while he was speaking. I fled far away, my heart beating, my arms failing, trembling had fallen on all my limbs. I turned about in running to seek a place to hide me, and I threw myself between two bushes, to wait while they should pass by.

Then I turned me toward the south, not from wishing to come into this palace--for I knew not if war was declared--nor even thinking a wish to live after this sovereign, I turned my back to the sycamore, I reached Shi-Seneferu, and rested on the open field. In the morning I went on and overtook a man, who passed by the edge of the road. He asked of me mercy, for he feared me. By the evening I drew near to Kher-ahau (? old Cairo), and I crossed the river on a raft without a rudder. Carried over by the west wind,

I passed over to the east to the quarries of Aku and the land of the goddess Herit, mistress of the red mountain (Gebel Ahmar). Then I fled on foot, northward, and reached the walls of the prince, built to repel the Sati. I crouched in a bush for fear of being seen by the guards, changed each day, who watch on the top of the fortress. I took my way by night, and at the lighting or the day I reached Peten, and turned me toward the valley of Kemur. Then thirst hasted me on; I dried up, and my throat narrowed, and I said, "This is the taste of death." When I lifted up my heart and gathered strength, I heard a voice and the lowing of cattle. I saw men of the Sati, and one of them--a friend unto Egypt--knew me. Behold he gave me water and boiled me milk, and I went with him to his camp; they did me good, and one tribe passed me on to another. I passed on to Sun, and reached the land of Adim (Edom). When I had dwelt there half a year Amu-an-shi--who is the prince of the Upper Tenu --sent for me and said: "Dwell thou with me that thou mayest hear the speech of Egypt." He said thus for that he knew of my excellence, and had heard tell of my worth, for men of Egypt who were there with him bore witness of me. Behold he said to me, "For what cause hast thou come hither? Has a matter come to pass in the palace? Has the king of the two lands, Sehetep-abra gone to heaven? That which has happened about this is not known." But I answered with concealment, and said, "When I came from the land of the Tamahu, and my desires were there changed in me, if I fled away it was not by reason of remorse that I took the way of a fugitive; I have not failed in my duty, my mouth has not said any bitter words, I have not heard any evil counsel, my name has not come into the mouth of a magistrate. I know not by what I have been led into this land." And Amu-an-shi said, "This is by the will of the god (king of Egypt), for what is a land like if it know not that excellent god, of whom the dread is upon the lands of strangers, as they dread Sekhet in a year of pestilence." I spake to him, and replied, "Forgive me, his son now enters the palace, and has received the heritage of his father. He is a god who has none like him, and there is none before him. He is a master of wisdom, prudent in his designs, excellent in his decrees, with good-will to him who goes or who comes; he subdued the land of strangers while his father yet lived in his palace, and he rendered account of that which his father destined him to perform. He is a brave

61

man, who verily strikes with his sword; a valiant one, who has not his equal; he springs upon the barbarians, and throws himself on the spoilers; he breaks the horns and weakens the hands, and those whom he smites cannot raise the buckler. He is fearless, and dashes the heads, and none can stand before him. He is swift of foot, to destroy him who flies; and none who flees from him reaches his home. His heart is strong in his time; he is a lion who strikes with the claw, and never has he turned his back. His heart is closed to pity; and when he sees multitudes, he leaves none to live behind him. He is a valiant one who springs in front when he sees resistance; he is a warrior who rejoices when he flies on the barbarians. He seizes the buckler, he rushes forward, he never needs to strike again, he slays and none can turn his lance; and when he takes the bow the barbarians flee from his arms like dogs; for the great goddess has given to him to strike those who know her not; and if he reaches forth he spares none, and leaves nought behind. He is a friend of great sweetness, who knows how to gain love; his land loves him more than itself, and rejoices in him more than in its own god; men and women run to his call. A king, he has ruled from his birth; he, from his birth, has increased births, a sole being, a divine essence, by whom this land rejoices to be governed. He enlarges the borders of the South , but he covets not the lands of the North; he does not smite the Sati, nor crush the Nemau-shau If he descends here, let him know thy name, by the homage which thou wilt pay to his majesty. For he refuses not to bless the land which obeys him." And he replied to me, "Egypt is indeed happy and well settled; behold thou art far from it, but whilst thou art with me I will do good unto thee." And he placed me before his children, he married his eldest daughter to me, and gave me the choice of all his land, even among the best of that which he had on the border of the next land. It is a goodly land, Iaa is its name. There are figs and grapes; there is wine commoner than water; abundant is the honey, many are its olives; and all fruits are upon its trees; there is barley and wheat, and cattle of kinds without end. This was truly a great thing that he granted me, when the prince came to invest me, and establish me as prince of a tribe in the best of his land. I had my continual portion of bread and of wine each day, of cooked meat, of roasted fowl, as well as the wild game which I took, or which was brought to me, besides what my dogs captured. They made me much butter, and prepared milk of all kinds. I passed many years, the children that I had became great, each ruling his tribe. When a messenger went or came to the palace, he turned aside from the way to come to me; for I helped every man. I gave water to the thirsty, I set on his way him who went astray, and I rescued the robbed. The Sati who went far, to strike and turn back the princes of other lands, I ordained their goings; for the Prince of the Tenu for many years appointed me to be general of his soldiers. In every land which I attacked I played the champion, I took the cattle, I led away the vassals, I carried off the slaves, I slew the people, by my sword, my bow, my marches and my good devices. I was excellent to the heart of my prince; he loved me when he knew my power, and set me over his children when he saw the strength of my arms. A champion of the Tenu came to defy me in my tent: a bold man without equal, for he had vanquished the whole country. He said, "Let Sanehat fight with me;" for he desired to overthrow me, he thought to take my cattle for his tribe. The prince councilled with me. I said, "I know him not. I certainly am not of his degree, I hold me far from his place. Have I ever opened his door, or leaped over his fence? It is some envious jealousy from seeing me; does he think that I am like some steer among the cows, whom the bull overthrows? If this is a wretch who thinks to enrich himself at my cost, not a Bedawi and a Bedawi fit for fight, then let us put the matter to judgment. Verily a true bull loves battle, but a vain-glorious bull turns his back for fear of contest; if he has a heart for combat, let him speak what he pleases. Will God forget what He has ordained, and how shall that be known?" I lay down; and when I had rested I strung my bow, I made ready my arrows, I loosened my poignard, I furbished my arms. At dawn the land of the Tenu came together; it had gathered its tribes and called all the neighbouring people, it spake of nothing but the fight. Each heart burnt for me, men and women crying out; for each heart was troubled for me, and they said, "Is there another strong one who would fight with him? Behold the adversary has a buckler, a battle axe, and an armful of javelins." Then I drew him to the attack; I turned aside his arrows, and they struck the ground in vain. One drew I near to the other, and he fell on me, and then I shot him. My arrow fastened in his neck, he cried out, and fell on his face: I drove his lance into him, and raised my shout of victory on his back. Whilst all the men of the land rejoiced, I, and his vassals whom he had oppressed, gave thanks unto Mentu. This prince, Amu-an-shi, embraced me. Then I carried off his goods and took his cattle, that which he had wished to do to me, I did even so unto him; I seized that which was in his tent, I spoiled his dwelling. As time went on I increased the richness of my treasures and the number of my cattle. Petition to the king of Egypt. "Now behold what the god has done for me who trusted in him. Having once fled away, yet now there is a witness of me in the palace. Once having fled away, as a fugitive,------now all in the palace give unto me a good name. After that I had been dying of hunger, now I give bread to those around. I had left my land naked, and now I am clothed in fine linen. After having been a wanderer without followers, now I possess many serfs. My house is fine, my land wide, my memory is established in the temple of all the gods. And let this flight obtain thy forgiveness; that I may be appointed in the palace; that I may see the place where my heart dwells. How great a thing is it that my body should be embalmed in the land where I was born! To return there is happiness. I have made offering to God, to grant me this thing. His heart suffers who has run away unto a strange land. Let him hear the prayer of him who is afar off, that he may revisit the place of his birth, and the place from which he removed. "May the king of Egypt be gracious to me that I may live of his favour. And I render my homage to the mistress of the land, who is in his palace; may I hear the news of her children. Thus will my limbs grow young again. Now old age comes, feebleness seizes me, my eyes are heavy, my arms are feeble, my legs will not move, my heart is slow. Death draws nigh to me, soon shall they lead me to the city of eternity. Let me follow the mistress of all (the queen, his former mistress); lo! let her tell me the excellencies of her children; may she bring eternity to me." Then the majesty of King Kheper-ka-ra, the blessed, spake upon this my desire that I had made to him. His majesty sent unto me with presents from the king, that he might enlarge the heart of his servant, like unto the province of any strange land; and the royal sons who are in the palace addressed themselves unto me. Copy of the decree which was brought--to me who speak to you--to lead me back into Egypt. "The Horus, life of births, lord of the crowns, life of births, king of Upper and Lower Egypt, Kheper-ka-ra, son of the Sun, Amen-em-hat, ever living unto eternity. Order for the follower Sanehat. Behold this order of the king is sent to thee to instruct thee of his will.

Now, although thou hast gone through strange lands from Adim to Tenu, and passed from one country to another at the wish of thy heart--behold, what hast thou done, or what has been done against thee, that is amiss? Moreover, thou reviledst not; but if thy word was denied, thou didst not speak again in the assembly of the nobles, even if thou wast desired. Now, therefore, that thou hast thought on this matter which has come to thy mind, let thy heart not change again; for this thy Heaven (queen), who is in the palace is fixed, she is flourishing, she is enjoying the best in the kingdom of the land, and her children are in the chambers of the palace. "Leave all the riches that thou hast, and that are with thee, altogether. When thou shalt come into Egypt behold the palace, and when thou shalt enter the palace, bow thy face to the ground before the Great House; thou shalt be chief among the companions. And day by day behold thou growest old; thy vigour is lost, and thou thinkest on the day of burial. Thou shalt see thyself come to the blessed state, they shall give thee the bandages from the hand of Tait, the night of applying the oil of embalming. They shall follow thy funeral, and visit the tomb on the day of burial, which shall be in a gilded case, the head painted with blue, a canopy of cypress wood above thee, and oxen shall draw thee, the singers going before thee, and they shall dance the funeral dance. The weepers crouching at the door of thy tomb shall cry aloud the prayers for offerings: they shall slay victims for thee at the door of thy pit; and thy pyramid shall be carved in white stone, in the company of the royal children. Thus thou shalt not die in a strange land, nor be buried by the Amu; thou shalt not be laid in a sheep-skin when thou art buried; all people shall beat the earth, and lament on thy body when thou goest to the tomb." When this order came to me, I was in the midst of my tribe. When it was read unto me, I threw me on the dust, I threw dust in my hair; I went around my tent rejoicing and saying, "How may it be that such a thing is done to the servant, who with a rebellious heart has fled to strange lands? Now with an excellent deliverance, and mercy delivering me from death, thou shall cause me to end my days in the palace." Copy of the answer to this order. "The follower Sanehat says: In excellent peace above everything consider of this flight that he made here in his ignorance; Thou, the Good God, Lord of both Lands, Loved of Ra, Favourite of Mentu, the lord of Thebes, and of Amen, lord of thrones of the lands, of Sebek, Ra, Horus, Hathor, Atmu, and of his fellow-gods, of Sopdu, Neferbiu, Samsetu, Horus, lord of the east, and of the royal uraeus which rules on thy head, of the chief gods of the waters, of Min, Horus of the desert, Urrit, mistress of Punt, Nut, Harnekht, Ra, all the gods of the land of Egypt, and of the isles of the sea. May they give life and peace to thy nostril, may they load thee with their gifts, may they give to thee eternity without end, everlastingness without bound. May the fear of thee be doubled in the lands of the deserts. Mayest thou subdue the circuit of the sun's disc. This is the prayer to his master of the humble servant who is saved from a foreign land. "O wise king, the wise words which are pronounced in the wisdom of the majesty of the sovereign, thy humble servant fears to tell. It is a great thing to repeat. O great God, like unto Ra in fulfilling that to which he has set his hand, what am I that he should take thought for me? Am I among those whom he regards, and for whom he arranges? Thy majesty is as Horus, and the strength of thy arms extends to all lands. "Then let his Majesty bring Maki of Adma,

Kenti-au-ush of Khenti-keshu, and Tenus from the two lands ol the Fenkhu; these are the princes who bear witness of me as to all that has passed, out of love for thyself. Does not Tenu believe that it belongs to thee like thy dogs. Behold this flight that I have made: I did not have it in my heart; it was like the leading of a dream, as a man of Adehi (Delta) sees himself in Abu (Elephantine), as a man of the plain of Egypt who sees himself in the deserts. There was no fear, there was no hastening after me, I did not listen to an evil plot, my name was not heard in the mouth of the magistrate; but my limbs went, my feet wandered, my heart drew me; my god commanded this flight, and drew me on; but I am not stiff-necked. Does a man fear when he sees his own land? Ra spread thy fear over the land, thy terrors in every strange land. Behold me now in the palace, behold me in this place; and lo! thou art he who is over all the horizon; the sun rises at thy pleasure, the water in the rivers is drunk at thy will, the wind in heaven is breathed at thy saying.

"I who speak to thee shall leave my goods to the generations to follow in this land. And as to this messenger who is come even let thy majesty do as pleaseth him, for one lives by the breath that thou givest. O thou who art beloved of Ra, of Horus, and of Hathor; Mentu, lord of Thebes, desires that thy august nostril should live for ever." I made a feast in Iaa, to pass over my goods to my children. My eldest son was leading my tribe, all my goods passed to him, and I gave him my corn and all my cattle, my fruit, and all my pleasant trees. When I had taken my road to the south, and arrived at the roads of Horus, the officer who was over the garrison sent a messenger to the palace to give notice. His majesty sent the good overseer of the peasants of the king's domains, and boats laden with presents from the king for the Sati who had come to conduct me to the roads of Horus. I spoke to each one by his name, and I gave the presents to each as was intended. I received and I returned the salutation, and I continued thus until I reached the city of Thetu. When the land was brightened, and the new day began, four men came with a summons for me; and the four men went to lead me to the palace. I saluted with both my hands on the ground; the royal children stood at the courtyard to conduct me: the courtiers who were to lead me to the hall brought me on the way to the royal chamber. I found his Majesty on the great throne in the hall of pale gold. Then I threw myself on my belly; this god, in whose presence I was, knew me not. He questioned me graciously, but I was as one seized with blindness, my spirit fainted, my limbs failed, my heart was no longer in my bosom, and I knew the difference between life and death. His majesty said to one of the companions,"Lift him up, let him speak to me." And his majesty said, "Behold thou hast come, thou hast trodden the deserts, thou hast played the wanderer. Decay falls on thee, old age has reached thee; it is no small thing that thy body should be embalmed, that the Pedtiu shall not bury thee. Do not, do not, be silent and speechless; tell thy name; is it fear that prevents thee?" I answered in reply, "I fear, what is it that my lord has said that I should answer it? I have not called on me the hand of God, but it is terror in my body, like that which brings sudden death. Now behold I am before thee; thou art life; let thy majesty do what pleaseth him." The royal children were brought in, and his majesty said to the queen, "Behold thou Sanehat has come as an Amu, whom the Sati have produced." She cried aloud, and the royal children spake with one voice, saying, before his majesty, "Verily it is not so, O king, my lord." Said his majesty, "It is verily he." Then they brought their collars, and their wands, and their sistra in their hands, and displayed them before his majesty; and they sang-- "May thy hands prosper, O king; May the ornaments of the Lady of Heaven continue. May the goddess Nub give life to thy nostril; May the mistress of the stars favour thee, when thou sailest south and north. All wisdom is in the mouth of thy majesty; Thy uraeus is on thy forehead, thou drivest away the miserable.

Thou art pacified, O Ra, lord of the lands; They call on thee as on the mistress of all. Strong is thy horn, Thou lettest fly thine arrow. Grant the breath to him who is without it; Grant good things to this traveller, Samehit the Pedti,

born in the land of Egypt, Who fled away from fear of thee, And fled this land from thy terrors. Does not the face grow pale, of him who beholds thy countenance; Docs not the eye fear, which looks upon thee."

Said his majesty, " Let him not fear, let him be freed from terror. He shall be a Royal Friend amongst the nobles; he shall be put within the circle of the courtiers. Go ye to the chamber of praise to seek wealth for him." When I went out from the palace, the royal children offered their hands to me; we walked afterwards to the

Great Gates. I was placed in a house of a king's son, in which were delicate things, a place of coolness, fruits of the granary, treasures of the White House, clothes of the king's guardrobe, frankincense, the finest perfumes of the king and the nobles whom he loves, in every chamber. All the servitors were in their several offices. Years were removed from my limbs: I was shaved, and polled my locks of hair; the foulness was cast to the desert with the garments of the Nemau-sha. I clothed me in fine linen, and anointed myself with the fine oil of Egypt; I laid me on a bed. I gave up the sand to those who lie on it; the oil of wood to him who would anoint himself therewith. There was given to me the mansion of a lord of serfs, which had belonged to a royal friend. There many excellent things were in its buildings; all its wood was renewed. There were brought to me portions from the palace, thrice and four times each day; besides the gifts of the royal children, always, without ceasing. There was built for me a pyramid of stone

amongst the pyramids. The overseer of the architects measured its ground; the chief treasurer wrote it; the sacred masons cut the well; the chief of the labourers on the tombs brought the bricks; all things used to make strong a building were there used. There were given to me peasants; there were made for me a garden, and fields in it before my mansion, as is done for the chief royal friend. My statue was inlayed with gold, its girdle of pale gold; his majesty caused it to be made. Such is not done to a man of low degree. May I be in the favour of the king until the day shall come of my death. (This is finished from beginning to end, as was found in the writing.)

REMARKS

The Adventures of Sanehat appears to have been a popular tale, as portions of three copies remain. The first papyrus known (Berlin No. I) was imperfect at the beginning; but since then a flake of limestone found in a tomb bore the beginning of the tale, and the same part is found on a papyrus in the Amherst collection. The main text has been translated by Chabas ("Le papyrus de Berlin," 37-51), Goodwin, and Maspero ("Mel. d'arch.," iii. 68, 140, and "Contes Populaire," 89-130); while the beginning is treated in "Memoires de l'institut Egyptien," ii. I-23, and in Proc. S.B.A., 452. The present translation is mainly based on Mr. Griffith's readings in all cases of difficulty. This is perhaps the most interesting of all the tales, because it bears such signs of being written in the times of which it treats, it throws so much light on the life of the time in Egypt and Syria, and if not a real narrative, it is at least so probable that it may be accepted without much difficulty. For my own part, I incline to look on it as strictly historical; and in the absence of a single point of doubt, I shall here treat it as seriously as the biographical inscriptions of the early tombs. Possibly some day the tomb of Sanehat may be found, and the whole inscription be read complete upon the walls. The name Sa-nehat means "son of the sycamore," probably from his having been born, or living, at some place where was a celebrated sacred sycamore. This was a common tree in ancient, as in modern, Egypt; but an allusion in the tale, to Sanehat turning his back on the sycamore, when he was fleeing apparently up the west side of the Delta, makes it probable that the sycamore was that of Aa-tenen, now Batnun, at the middle of the west side of the Delta. The titles given to Sanehat at the opening are of a very high rank, and imply that he was the son either of the king or of a great noble. And his position in the queen's household shows him to have been of importance; the manner in which he is received by the royal family at the end implying that he was quite familiar with them in early days. But the great difficulty in the account has been the sudden panic of Sanehat on hearing of the death of Amenemhat, and no explanation of this has yet been brought forward. It seems not unlikely that he was a son of Amenemhat by some concubine. This would at once account for his high titles--for his belonging to the royal household--for his fear of his elder brother Usertesen, who might see in him a rival, and try to slay him after his father's death--for the command to him to leave all his possessions and family behind him in Syria, as the condition of his being allowed to return to end his days in Egypt--for his familiar reception by the royal family, and for the property given to him on his return. The date recorded for the death of Sehote-pabra--Amenemhat I., the founder of the XIIth Dynasty--agrees with the limit of his reign on the monuments. And the expressions for his death are valuable as showing the manner in which a king's decease was regarded; under the emblem of a hawk--the bird of Ra--he flew up and joined the sun. Sometime before his death Amenemhat had been in retirement; after twenty years of reign (which was probably rather late in

his life, as he seems to have forced his way to the
front as a successful man and founder of a family)
he had associated his son, the first Usertesen, on
the throne, and apparently resigned active life; for
in the third year of Usertesen we find the
coregent summoning his court and decreeing the
founding of the temple of Heliopolis without
any mention of his father. The old king, however,
lived yet ten years after his retirement, and died
(as this narrative shows us) during an expedition
of his son Usertesen. The time of year mentioned
here would fall in about the middle of the
inundation in those days. Hence it seems that the
military expeditions were made after the harvest
was secured, and while the country was under
water and the population disengaged from other
labour. The course of Sanehat's flight southward,
reaching the Nile at Cairo after two days' haste,
indicates that the army was somewhere west of
the Delta. This would point to its being on the
road to the oasis of the Natron Lakes, which
would be the natural course for a body of men
needing water supply. His throwing himself
between two bushes to hide from the army shows
that the message came early in the day, otherwise
he would have fled in the dark. He then fled a
day's journey to the south, turning his back on

the sycamore, and slept in the open field at Shi-Seneferu somewhere below the Barrage. The second day he reached the Nile opposite Old Cairo in the afternoon, and ferried himself over, passed the quarries at Gebel Mokattam, and the red hill of Gebel Ahmar, and came to a frontier wall before dark. This cannot have been far from Old Cairo, by the time; and as Heliopolis was in course of building by Usertesen, it would be probably on the desert near there, for the protection of the town. Passing the desert guards by night he pushed on and reached Peten, near Belbeis, by dawn, and turned east toward the valley of Kemur, or Wady Tumilat. Here in his extremity he was found by the Sati or Asiatics, and rescued. This shows that the eastern desert was left to the wandering tribes, and was without any regular government at this period; though all the eastern Delta was already well in Egyptian hands, as we know by the monuments at Bubastis, Dedamun, and Tanis. The land of Adim to which Sanehat fled appears to be the same as Edom or the southeast corner of Syria. It was evidently near the upper Tenu, or Rutennu, who seem to have dwelt on the hill country of Palestine. The hill and the plain of Palestine are so markedly different, that in all ages they have tended to be held by opposing people. In the time of Sanehat the upper Tenu who held the hills were opposed to the Tenu in general who held the plains; later on the Semites of the hills opposed the Philistines of the plain, and now the fellah of the hills opposes the Bedawi of the plain. The district of Amuanshi in which Sanehat settled was a goodly land, bearing figs and grapes and olives, flowing with wine and honey and oil, yielding barley and wheat without end, and much cattle. This abundance points rather to the hill country near Hebron or between there and Belt Jibrin, as this south part of the hills is notably fertile. The Tenu who came to defy Sanehat, being in opposition to the upper Tenu, were probably those of the plain; and the opposition to Sanehat may have arisen from his encroaching on the fertile plain at the foot of his hills, as he was in the best of the land "on the border of the next land." The Egyptian was evidently looked on as being of a superior race by the Tenu, and his civilisation won for him the confidence which many wandering Englishmen now find in Africa or Polynesia, like John Dunn. The set combat of two champions seems--by the large gathering--to have been a well-recognised custom among the Tenu, while it exactly accords with Goliath's offer in later times. And raising the shout of victory on the back of the fallen champion reminds us of David's standing on Goliath. The transition from the recital of the Syrian adventures to the petition to Pharaoh is not marked in the manuscript; but from the construction the beginning of the petition is evidently at the place here marked. The manner in which Sanehat appeals to the queen shows how well he must have been known to her in his former days. The decree in reply to Sanehat is in the regular style of royal decrees of the period. Apparently by a clerical error the scribe has substituted the name Amenemhat for Userte-sen, but the Horus name and the throne name leave no doubt that Usertesen I. is intended here. The tone of the reply is as gracious as possible, according with the king's character as stated by Sanehat, "He is a friend of great sweetness, and knows how to gain love." He quite recognises the inquiries after the queen, and replies concerning her. And then he assures Sanehat of welcome on his return, and promises him all that he asks, including a tomb "in the company of the royal children," a full recognition of his real rank. Incidentally we learn that the Amu buried their dead wrapped in a sheep's skin; as we also learn, further on, that they anointed themselves with oil (olive?), wore the hair long, and slept on the ground. The funeral that is promised accords with the burials of the XIIth Dynasty: the gilded case, the head painted blue, and the canopy of cypress wood, are all known of this period, but would be out of place in describing a Ramesside burial. Sanehat's reply is a full course of the usual

religious adulation, and differs in this remarkably from his petition. In fact it is hard to be certain where his petition begins; possibly the opening of it has been lost out of the text in copying from a mutilated papyrus; or possibly it was sent merely as a memorandum of Sanehat's position and desires, without venturing to address it personally to the king; or even it may have not been allowable then to make such petitions formally, so as to leave the initiative to the king's free will, just as it is not allowable nowadays to question royalty, but only to answer when spoken to. The proposal to bring forward his fellow-sheikhs as witnesses of his unabated loyalty is very curious, and seems superfluous after Usertesen's assurances. Beyond Abisha of the Amu at Beni Hasan, these are the only early personal names of Syrians that we know. The Fenkhu in this connection can hardly be other than the Phoenicians; and, if so, this points to their being already established in southern Syria at this date. But these chiefs were not allowed to come forward; and it seems to have been the policy of Egypt to keep the Syrians off as much as possible, not a single man who came with Sanehat being allowed to cross the frontier. The allusion to the Tenu belonging to Pharaoh, like his dogs, is peculiarly fitting to this period, as the dog seems to have been more familiarly domesticated in the XIth and XIIth Dynasties than at any other age, and dogs are often then represented on the funereal steles, even with their names. The expression for strangeness--"as a man of the Delta sees himself at the cataract, as a man of the plain who sees himself in the deserts"--is true to this day. Nothing upsets an Egyptian's self-reliance like going back a few miles into the desert; and almost any man of the cultivated plain will flee with terror if he finds himself left alone far in the desert, or even taken to the top of the desert hills. .

We learn incidentally that the Egyptian frontier, even in the later years of Usertesen I., had not been pushed beyond the Wady Tumilat; for Sanehat travels south to the Roads of Horus, where he finds the frontier garrison, and leaves his Syrian friends; and there laden boats meet him, showing that it must have been somewhere along a waterway from the Nile. The abasement of Sanehat might well be due to natural causes, beside the reverence for the divine person of the king. The Egyptian court must have seemed oppressively splendid, with the brilliant and costly workmanship of Usertesen, to one who had lived a half-wild life for so many years; and, more than that, the recalling of all his early days and habits and friendships would overwhelm his mind and make it difficult to collect his thoughts. Sanehat's appearance was so much changed by his long hair, his age, and his strange dress, that his former mistress and companions could not recognise him. The use of collars and sceptres in the song and dance is not clear to us. The sistra were, of course, to beat or rattle in time with the song; the sceptres or wands were perhaps the same as the engraved wands of ivory common in the XIIth Dynasty, or of blue glazed ware in XVIIIth, and would be used to wave or beat time with; but the use of the collar and counterpoise, or menat, is unexplained, though figures of dancers are shown holding a collar and menat, and such objects were found buried in the ceremonial foundation deposit of Tahutmes III.

at Koptos. This song of the princesses is clearly in parallel phrases. First are four wishes for the king and queen, in four lines. Second, an ascription of wisdom and power, in two lines. Third, a comparison of the king to Ra, and of the queen to the great goddess, in two lines. Fourth, an ascription of righting power. Fifth, a petition for Sanehat, winding up with the statement of fear inspired by the king, as explaining Sanehat's abasement. To this the king responds by reassuring Sanehat, and promising him position and wealth. The account of Sanehat's renewal of his old national ways can best be appreciated by any one who has lived a rough life for a time and then comes back to civilisation. Doubtless these comforts were all the more grateful to him in his old age, when he was weary of his unsettled life. In the preparation of his tomb it is stated to have been a pyramid, with rock-cut well chamber, and built of bricks above. This just accords with the construction of the pyramids of the XIIth Dynasty. The last phrase implies that this was composed during Sanehat's life; and such a life would be so remarkable that this biography might be prepared with good reason. Also it is very unlikely that a mere story-teller would have dropped the relation without describing his grand funeral which was promised to him. From suddenly stopping at the preparation of the tomb, without going further, we have a strong presumption that this was a true narrative, written at Sanehat's dictation, and probably intended to be inscribed on his tomb wall. In any case, we have here an invaluable picture of life in Palestine and in Egypt, and the relations of the two countries, at an epoch before the time of Abraham, and not paralleled by any other document until more than a thousand years later.

EGYPTIAN TALES

TRANSLATED FROM THE PAPYRI

SECOND SERIES
XVIIIth TO XIXth DYNASTY

EDITED BY
W. M. FLINDERS PETRIE,
HON. D.C.L., LL.D.
EDWARDS PROFESSOR OF EGYPTOLOGY, UNIVERSITY
COLLEGE, LONDON

PREFACE

AS the scope of the first series of these Tales seems to have been somewhat overlooked, a few words of introduction may not be out of place before this second volume.

It seems that any simple form of fiction is supposed to be a "fairy tale:" which implies that it has to do with an impossible world of imaginary beings. Now the Egyptian Tales are exactly the opposite of this, they relate the doings and the thoughts of men and women who are human--sometimes "very human," as Mr. Balfour said. Whatever there is of supernatural elements is a very part of the beliefs and motives of the people whose lives are here pictured. But most of what is here might happen in some corner of our own country to-day, where ancient beliefs may have a home. So far, then, from being fairy tales there is not a single being that could be termed a fairy in the whole of them.

Another notion that seems to be about is that the only possible object of reading any form of fiction is for pure amusement, to fill an idle hour and be forgotten and if these tales are not as amusing as some jester of to-day, then the idler says, Away with them as a failure! For such a person, who only looks to have the tedium of a vacuous mind relieved, these tales are not in the least intended. But the real and genuine charm of all fiction is that of enabling the reader to place himself in the mental position of, another, to see with the eyes, to feel with the thoughts, to reason with the mind, of a wholly different being. All the greatest work has this charm. It may be to place the reader in new mental positions, or in a different level of the society that he already knows, either higher or lower; or it may be to make alive to him a society of a different land or age. Whether he read "Treasure Island" or "Plain Tales from the Hills," "The Scarlet Letter," "Old Mortality," or "Hypatia," it is the transplanting of the reader into a new life, the doubling of his mental experience, that is the very power of fiction. The same interest attaches to these tales. In place of regarding Egyptians only as the builders of pyramids and the makers of mummies, we here see the men and women as they lived, their passions, their foibles, their beliefs, and their follies. The old refugee Sanehat craving to be buried with his ancestors in the blessed land, the enterprise and success of the Doomed Prince, the sweetness of Bata, the misfortunes of Ahura, these all live before us, and we can for a brief half hour share the feelings and see with the eyes of those who ruled the world when it was young. This is the real value of these tales, and the power which still belongs to the oldest literature in the world.

XVIIITH DYNASTY

THE TAKING OF JOPPA

THERE was once in the time of King
Men-kheper-ra a revolt of the servants of his
majesty who were in Joppa; and his majesty said,
"Let Tahutia go with his footmen and destroy
this wicked Foe in Joppa." And he called one of
his followers, and said moreover, "Hide thou my
great cane, which works wonders, in the baggage
of Tahutia that my power may go with him."

Now when Tahutia came near to Joppa,
with all the footmen of Pharaoh, he sent unto the
Foe in Joppa, and said, "Behold now his majesty,
King Men-kheper-ra, has sent all this great army
against thee; but what is that if my heart is as thy
heart? Do thou come, and let us talk in the field,
and see each other face to face." So Tahutia came
with certain of his men; and the Foe in Joppa
came likewise, but his charioteer that was with
him was true of heart unto the king of Egypt.
And they spoke with one another in his great
tent, which Tahutia had placed far off from the

soldiers. But Tahutia had made ready two hundred sacks, with cords and fetters, and had made a great sack of skins with bronze fetters, and many baskets: and they were in his tent, the sacks and the baskets, and he had placed them as the forage for the horses is put in baskets. For whilst the Foe in Joppa drank with Tahutia, the people who were with him drank with the footmen of Pharaoh, and made merry with them. And when their bout of drinking was past, Tahutia said to the Foe in Joppa, "If it please thee, while I remain with the women and children of thy own city, let one bring of my people with their horses, that they may give them provender, or let one of the Apuro run to fetch them." So they came, and hobbled their horses, and gave them provender, and one found the great cane of Men-kheper-ra (Tahutmes III.), and came to tell of it to Tahutia. And thereupon the Foe in Joppa said to Tahutia, "My heart is set on examining the great cane of Men-kheper-ra, which is named '. . . tautnefer.' By the ka of the King Men-kheper-ra it will be in thy hands to-day; now do thou well and bring thou it to me." And Tahutia did thus, and he brought the cane of King Men-kheper-ra. And he laid hold on the Foe in Joppa by his garment, and he arose and stood up, and said, "Look on me, O Foe in Joppa; here is the great cane of King Men-kheper-ra, the terrible lion, the son of Sekhet, to whom Amen his father gives power and strength."

And he raised his hand and struck the forehead of the Foe in Joppa, and he fell helpless before him. He put him in the sack of skins and he bound with gyves the hands of the Foe in Joppa, and put on his feet the fetters with four rings. And he made

them bring the two hundred sacks which he had cleaned, and made to enter into them two hundred soldiers, and filled the hollows with cords and fetters of wood, he sealed them with a seal, and added to them their rope-nets and the poles to bear them. And he put every strong footman to bear them, in all six hundred men, and said to them, "When you come into the town you shall open your burdens, you shall seize on all the inhabitants of the town, and you shall quickly put fetters upon them,"

Then one went out and said unto the charioteer of the Foe in Joppa, "Thy master is fallen; go, say to thy mistress, 'A pleasant message! For Sutekh has given Tahutia to us, with his wife and his children; behold the beginning of their tribute,' that she may comprehend the two hundred sacks, which are full of men and cords and fetters." So he went before them to please the heart of his mistress, saying, "We have laid hands on Tahutia." Then the gates of the city were opened before the footmen: they entered the city, they opened their burdens, they laid hands on them of the city, both small and great, they put on them the cords and fetters quickly; the power of Pharaoh seized upon that city. After he had rested Tahutia sent a message to Egypt to the King Men-kheper-ra his lord, saying, "Be pleased, for Amen thy good father has given to thee the Foe in Joppa, together with all his people, likewise also his city. Send, therefore, people to take them as captives that thou mayest fill the house of thy father Amen Ra, king of the gods, with men-servants and maid-servants, and that they may be overthrown beneath thy feet for ever and ever."

REMARKS

This tale of the taking of Joppa appears to be probably on an historical basis. Tahutia was a well-known officer of Tahutmes III.; and the splendid embossed dish of weighty gold which the king presented to him is one of the principal treasures of the Louvre museum. It is ornamented with groups of fish in the flat bottom, and a long inscription around the side.

Unfortunately the earlier part of this tale has been lost; but in order to render it intelligible I have restored an opening to it, without introducing any details but what are alluded to, or necessitated, by the existing story.

It is evident that the basis of the tale is the stratagem of the Egyptian general, offering to make friends with the rebel of Joppa, while he sought to trap him. To a Western soldier such an unblushing offer of being treacherous to his master the king would be enough to make the good faith of his proposals to the enemy very doubtful. But in the East offers of wholesale desertion are not rare. In Greek history it was quite an open question whether Athens or Persia would retain a general's service; in Byzantine history a commander might be in favour with the Khalif one year and with the Autokrator the next; and in the present century the entire transfer of the Turkish fleet to Mohammed Ali in 1840 is a grand instance of such a case.

The scheme of taking a fortress by means of smuggling in soldiers hidden in packages has often recurred in history; but this taking of Joppa is the oldest tale of the kind yet known. Following this we have the wooden horse of Troy. Then comes in mediaeval times the Arab scheme for taking Edessa, in 1038 A.D., by a train of five hundred camels bearing presents for the Autokrator at Constantinople. The governor of Edessa declined to admit such travellers, and a bystander, hearing some talking in the baskets slung on the camels, soon gave the alarm, which led to the destruction of the whole party; the chief alone, less hands, ears, and nose, being left to take the tale back to Bagdad. And in fiction there are the stories of a lady avenging her husband by introducing men hidden in skins, and the best known version of all in the "Arabian Nights," of Ali Baba and the thieves.

It appears from the tale that the conference of Tahutia with the rebel took place between the town and the Egyptian army, but near the town. Then Tahutia proposes to go into the town as a pledge of his sincerity, while the men of the town were to supply his troops with fodder. But he appears to have remained talking with the rebel in the tent, until the lucky chance of the stick turned up. This cleared the way for a neater management of his plan, by enabling him to quietly make away with the chief, without exciting his suspicions beforehand.

The name of the cane of the king is partly illegible; but we know how many actual sticks and personal objects have their own names inscribed on them. Nothing had a real entity to the Egyptian mind without an individual name belonging to it.

The message sent by the charioteer presupposes that he was in the secret; and he must therefore have been an Egyptian who had not heartily joined in the rebellion. From the conclusion we see that the captives taken as slaves to Egypt were by no means only prisoners of war, but were the ordinary civil inhabitants of the conquered cities, "them of the city, both small and great."

The gold dish which the king gave to the tomb of Tahuti is so splendid that it deserves some notice, especially as it has never been published in England. It is circular, about seven inches across, with vertical sides an inch high. The inside of the bottom bears a boss and rosette in the centre, a line of swimming fish around that, and beyond all a chain of lotus flowers. On the upright edge is an incised inscription, "Given in praise by the king of Upper and Lower Egypt, Ra-men-kheper, to the hereditary chief, the divine father, the beloved by God, filling the heart of the king in all foreign lands and in the isles in the midst of the great sea, filling stores with lazuli, electrum, and gold, keeper of all foreign lands, keeper of the troops, praised by the good gold lord of both lands and his ka,--the royal scribe Tahuti deceased." This splendid piece of gold work was therefore given in honour of Tahuti at his funeral, to be placed in his tomb for the use of his ka. The weight of it is very nearly a troy pound, being 5,729 grains or four utens. The allusion on it to the Mediterranean wars of Tahuti, "satisfying the king in all foreign lands and in the isles in the midst of the great sea," is just in accord with this tale of the conquest of Joppa.

Beside this golden bowl there are many other objects from Tahuti's tomb which must have been very rich, and have escaped plundering until this century. A silver dish, broken, and a canopic jar of alabaster, are in Paris; another canopic jar, a palette, a kohl vase, and a heart scarab set in gold, are in Leyden; while in Darmstadt is the dagger of this great general. This piece of a popular tale founded on an incident of his Syrian wars has curiously survived, while the more solid official records of his conquests has perished in the wreck of history. His tomb even is unknown, although it has been plundered; perhaps his active life of foreign service did not give him that leisure to carve and decorate it, which was so laboriously spent by the home-living dignitaries of Thebes,

CLOSE OF THE XVIIIth DYNASTY

THE DOOMED PRINCE

THERE once was a king to whom no son was born; and his heart was grieved, and he prayed for himself unto the gods around him for a child. They decreed that one should be born to him. And his wife, after her time was fulfilled, brought forth a son. Then came the Hathors to decree for him a destiny; they said, "His death is to be by the crocodile, or by the serpent, or by the dog." Then the people who stood by heard this, and they went to tell it to his majesty. Then his majesty's heart sickened very greatly. And his majesty caused a house to be built upon the desert; it was furnished with people and with all

good things of the royal house, that the child should not go abroad. And when the child was grown, he went up upon the roof, and he saw a dog; it was following a man who was walking on the road. He spoke to his page, who was with him, "What is this that walks behind the man who is coming along the road?" He answered him, "This is a dog." The child said to him, "Let there be brought to me one like it." The page went to repeat it to his majesty. And his majesty said, "Let there be brought to him a little pet dog, lest his heart be sad." And behold they brought to him the dog.

Then when the days increased after this, and when the child became grown in all his limbs, he sent a message to his father saying, "Come, wherefore am I kept here? Inasmuch as I am fated to three evil fates, let me follow my desire. Let God do what is in His heart." They agreed to all he said, and gave him all sorts of arms, and also his dog to follow him, and they took him to the east country, and said to him, "Behold, go thou whither thou wilt." His dog was with him, and he went northward, following his heart in the desert, while he lived on all the best of the game of the desert. He went to the chief of Naha-raina.

And behold there had not been any born to the chief of Naharaina, except one daughter. Behold, there had been built for her a house; its seventy windows were seventy cubits from the ground. And the chief caused to be brought all the sons of the chiefs of the land of Khalu, and said to them, "He who reaches the window of my daughter, she shall be to him for a wife."

And many days after these things, as they were in their daily task, the youth rode by the place where they were. They took the youth to their house, they bathed him, they gave provender to his horses, they brought all kinds of things for the youth, they perfumed him, they anointed his feet, they gave him portions of their own food; and they spake to him, "Whence comest thou, goodly youth?" He said to them, "I am son of an officer of the land of Egypt; my mother is dead, and my father has taken another wife. And when she bore children, she grew to hate me, and I have come as a fugitive from before her." And they embraced him, and kissed him.

And after many days were passed, he said to the youths, "What is it that ye do here?" And they said to him, "We spend our time in this: we climb up, and he who shall reach the window of the daughter of the chief of Naharaina, to him will he given her to wife." He said to them, "If it please you, let me behold the matter, that I may come to climb with you." They went to climb, as was their daily wont: and the youth stood afar off to behold; and the face of the daughter of the chief of Naharaina was turned to them. And another day the sons came to climb, and the youth came to climb with the sons of the chiefs. He climbed, and he reached the window of the daughter of the chief of Naharaina. She kissed him, she embraced him in all his limbs.

And one went to rejoice the heart of her father, and said to him, "One of the people has reached the window of thy daughter." And the prince inquired of the messenger, saying, "The son of which of the princes is it?" And he replied to him, "It is the son of an officer, who has come as a fugitive from the land of Egypt, fleeing from before his stepmother when she had children." Then the chief of Naharaina was exceeding angry; and he said, "Shall I indeed give my daughter to the Egyptian fugitive?

Let him go back whence he came." And one came to tell the youth, "Go back to the place thou earnest from." But the maiden seized his hand; she swore an oath by God, saying, "By the being of Ra Harakhti, if one takes him from me, I will not eat, I will not drink, I shall die in that same hour." The messenger went to tell unto her father all that she said. Then the prince sent men to slay the youth, while he was in his house. But the maiden said, "By the being of Ra, if one slay him I shall be dead ere the sun goeth down. I will not pass an hour of life if I am parted from him." And one went to tell her father. Then the prince made them bring the youth with the maiden. The youth was seized with fear when he came before the prince. But he embraced him, he kissed him all over, and said, "Oh! tell me who thou art; behold, thou art to me as a son." He said to him, "I am a son of an officer of the land of Egypt; my mother died, my father took to him a second wife; she came to hate me, and I fled a fugitive from before her." He then gave to him his daughter to wife; he gave also to him a house, and serfs, and fields, also cattle and all manner of good things.

But after the days of these things were passed, the youth said to his wife, "I am doomed to three fates--a crocodile, a serpent, and a dog." She said to him, "Let one kill the dog which belongs to thee." He replied to her, "I am not going to kill my dog, which I have brought up from when it was small." And she feared greatly for her husband, and would not let him go alone abroad.

And one went with the youth toward the land of Egypt, to travel in that country. Behold the crocodile of the river, he came out by the town in which the youth was. And in that town was a mighty man. And the mighty man would not suffer the crocodile to escape. And when the crocodile was bound, the mighty man went out and walked abroad. And when the sun rose the mighty man went back to the house; and he did so every day, during two months of days.

Now when the days passed after this, the youth sat making a good day in his house.

And when the evening came he lay down on his bed, sleep seized upon his limbs; and his wife filled a bowl of milk, and placed it by his side. Then came out a serpent from his hole, to bite the youth; behold his wife was sitting by him, she lay not down. Thereupon the servants gave milk to the serpent, and he drank, and was drunk, and lay upside down. Then his wife made it to perish with the blows of her dagger. And they woke her husband, who was astonished; and she said unto him, "Behold thy God has given one of thy dooms into thy hand; He will also give thee the others." And he sacrificed to God, adoring Him, and praising His spirits from day to day.

And when the days were passed after these things, the youth went to walk in the fields of his domain. He went not alone, behold his dog was following him. And his dog ran aside after the wild game, and he followed the dog. He came to the river, and entered the river behind his dog. Then came out the crocodile, and took him to the place where the mighty man was. And the crocodile said to the youth, "I am thy doom, following after thee. ..."

[Here the papyrus breaks off.]

REMARKS

This tale is preserved in one of the Harris papyri (No. 500) in the British Museum. It has been translated by Goodwin, Chabas, Maspero, and Ebers. The present version is adapted from that of Maspero, with frequent reference by Mr. Griffith to the original.

The marvellous parentage of a fated or gifted hero is familiar in Eastern tales, and he is often described as a divine reward to a long-childless king. This element of fate or destiny is, however, not seen before this age in Egyptian ideas; nor, indeed, would it seem at all in place with the simple, easygoing, joyous life of the early days. It belongs to an age when ideals possess the mind, when man struggles against his circumstances, when he wills to be different from what he is. Dedi or the shipwrecked sailor think nothing about fate, but live day by day as life comes to them. There is here, then, a new element, that of striving and of unrest, quite foreign to the old Egyptian mind. The age of this tale is shown plainly in the incidents. The prince goes to the chief of Naharaina, a land probably unknown to the Egyptians until the Asiatic conquests of the XVIIIth Dynasty had led them to the upper waters of the Euphrates. In earlier days Sanehat fled to the frontier at the Wady Tumilat, and was quite lost to Egypt when he settled in the south of Palestine. But when the Doomed Prince goes out of Egypt he goes to the chief of Naharaina, as the frontier State. This stamps the tale as subsequent to the wars of the Tahutimes family, and reflects rather the peaceful intercourse of the great monarch Amenhotep the Third. If it belonged to the Ramessides we should not hear of Naharaina, which was quite lost to them, but rather of Dapur (Tabor) and Kadesh, and of the Hittites as the familiar frontier power.

The Hathors here appear as the Fates, instead of the goddesses Isis, Nebhat, Mes-khent, and Hakt, of the old tale in the IVth Dynasty (see first series, p. 33); and we find in the next tale of Anpu and Bata, in the XIXth Dynasty, that the seven Hathors decree the fate of the wife of Bata. That Hathor should be a name given to seven deities is not strange when we see that Hathor was a generic name for a goddess. There was the Hathor of foreign lands, such as Punt or Sinai; there was the Hathor of home towns, as Dendera or Atfih; and Hathor was as widely known, and yet as local, as the Madonna. In short, to one of the races which composed the Egyptian people Hathor was the term for any goddess, or for a universal goddess to whom all others were assimilated. Why and how this title "house of Horus " should be so general is not obvious.

The variety of fate here predicted is like the vagueness of the fate of Bata's wife, by "a sharp death." It points to the Hathors predicting as seers, rather than to their having the control of the future. It bears the stamp of the oracle of Delphi, rather than that of a divine decree. In this these goddesses differ greatly from the Parcae, whose ordinances not even Zeus could withstand, as Lucian lets us know in one of the most audacious and philosophical of the dialogues. The Hathors seem rather to deal with what we should call luck than with fate: they see the nature of the close of life from its beginning, without either knowing or controlling its details.

In this tale we meet for the first time the idea of inaccessible and mysterious buildings; and from the resort to this element or curiosity in describing both the prince and the princess, it appears as if it were then a new motive in story-telling, and had not lost its power. To modern ears it is, of course, done to death since the "Castle of Otranto"; though as a minor element it can still be gently used by the poet and novelist in a moated grange, a house in a marsh or a maze. Another point of wonder, so well known in later times, is the large and mystic number of windows, like the 365 windows attributed to great buildings of the present age. It would not be difficult from these papyrus tales to start an historical dictionary of the elements of fiction: a kind of analysis that should be the death of much of the venerable stock-in-trade.

We see coming in here, more strongly than before, the use of emotions and the force of character. The generous friendship of the sons of the Syrian chiefs; then the burst of passionate love from the chiefs daughter, which saves the prince's life twice over from her father, and guards him afterwards from his fates; again, the devotion of the prince to his favourite dog, in spite of all warnings--these show a reliance on personal emotion and feeling in creating the interest of the tale, quite different from the mere interest of incident which was employed earlier. The reason which the prince alleges for his leaving Egypt is also a touch of nature, the wish of a mother to oust her stepson in order to make way for her own children, one of the deepest and most elemental feelings of feminine nature.

The mighty man and the crocodile are difficult to understand, the more so as the tale breaks off in the midst of that part. It appears also as if there had been some inversion of the paragraphs; for, first, we read that the wife would not let the prince go alone, and one goes with him toward Egypt, and the crocodile of the Nile (apparently) is mentioned; then he is said to be sitting in his house with his wife; then he goes in the fields of his domain and meets the crocodile. It may be that a passage has dropped out, describing his wife's accompanying him to settle in Egypt. But the mighty man--that is another puzzle. He binds a crocodile, and goes out while he is bound, but by night. The point of this is not clear. It may have been, however, that the mighty man went back to the house when the sun was high, that he might not lose his shadow. In Arabia there was a belief that a hyasna could deprive a man of speech and motion by stepping on his shadow--analogous to the belief in many other lands of the importance of preserving the shadow, and avoiding the shadowless hour of high noon (Frazer, "Golden Bough," p. 143). Hence the strength of the mighty man, and his magic power over the crocodile, would perhaps depend on his not allowing his shadow to disappear. And though Egypt is not quite tropical, yet shadows do practically vanish in the summer, the shadow of the thin branches of a tall palm appearing to radiate round its root without the stem casting any shade.

The use of milk to entice serpents is still well known in Egypt; and when a serpent appeared in some of my excavations in a pit, the men proposed to me to let down a saucer of milk to entice it out, that they might kill it.

The close of the tale would have explained much that is now lost to us. The crocodile boasts of being the fate of the prince; but his dog is with him, and one can hardly doubt that the dog attacks the crocodile. There is also the mighty man to come in and manage the crocodile. Then the dog is left to bring about the catastrophe. Or does the faithful wife rescue him from all the fates? Hardly so, as the prediction of the Hathors comes strictly to pass in the tale of Anpu and Bata. Let us hope that another copy may be found to give us the clue to the working of the Egyptian mind in this situation.

XIXTH DYNASTY

ANPU AND BATA.

ONCE there were two brethren, of one mother and one father; Anpu was the name of the elder, and Bata was the name of the younger. Now, as for Anpu he had a house, and he had a wife. But his little brother was to him as it were a son; he it was who made for him his clothes; he it was who followed behind his oxen to the fields; he it was who did the ploughing; he it was who harvested the corn; he it was who did for him all the matters that were in the field. Behold, his younger brother grew to be an excellent worker, there was not his equal in the whole land; behold, the spirit of a god was in him.

Now after this the younger brother followed his oxen in his daily manner; and every evening he turned again to the house, laden with all the herbs of the field, with milk and with wood, and with all things of the field. And he put them down before his elder brother, who was sitting with his wife; and he drank and ate, and he lay down in his stable with the cattle. And at the dawn of day he took bread which he had baked, and laid it before his elder brother; and he took with him his bread to the field, and he drave his cattle to pasture in the fields. And as he walked behind his cattle, they said to him, "Good is the herbage which is in that place; " and he listened to all that they said, and he took them to the good place which they desired. And the cattle which were before him became exceeding excellent, and they multiplied greatly.

Now at the time of ploughing his elder brother said unto him, "Let us make ready for ourselves a goodly yoke of oxen for ploughing, for the land has come out from the water, it is fit for ploughing. Moreover, do thou come to the field with corn, for we will begin the ploughing in the morrow morning." Thus said he to him; and his younger brother did all things as his elder brother had spoken unto him to do them.

And when the morn was come, they went to the fields with their things; and their hearts were pleased exceedingly with their task in the beginning of their work. And it came to pass after this that as they were in the field they stopped for corn, and he sent his younger brother, saying, "Haste thou, bring to us corn from the farm." And the younger brother found the wife of his elder brother, as she was sitting tiring her hair. He said to her, "Get up, and give to me corn, that I may run to the field, for my elder brother hastened me; do not delay." She said to him, "Go, open the bin, and thou shalt take to thyself according to thy will, that I may not drop my locks of hair while I dress them."

The youth went into the stable; he took a large measure, for he desired to take much corn; he loaded it with wheat and barley; and he went out carrying it. She said to him, "How much of the corn that is wanted, is that which is on thy shoulder?" He said to her, "Three bushels of barley, and two of wheat, in all five; these are what are upon my shoulder: " thus said he to her. And she conversed with him, saying, "There is great strength in thee, for I see thy might every day." And her heart knew him with the knowledge of youth. And she arose and came to him, and conversed with him, saying, "Come, stay with me, and it shall be well for thee, and I will make for thee beautiful garments." Then the youth became like a panther of the south with fury at the evil speech which she had made to him; and she feared greatly. And he spake unto her, saying, "Behold thou art to me as a mother, thy husband is to me as a father, for he who is elder than I has brought me up. What is this wickedness that thou hast said to me? Say it not to me again. For I will not tell it to any man, for I will not let it be uttered by the mouth of any man." He lifted up his burden, and he went to the field and came to his elder brother; and they took up their work, to labour at their task.

Now afterward, at eventime, his elder brother was returning to his house; and the younger brother was following after his oxen, and he loaded himself with all the things of the field; and he brought his oxen before him, to make them lie down in their stable which was in the farm. And behold the wife of the elder brother was afraid for the words which she had said. She took a parcel of fat, she became like one who is evilly beaten, desiring to say to her husband, "It is thy younger brother who has done this wrong." Her husband returned in the even, as was his wont of every day; he came unto his house; he found his wife ill of violence; she did not give him water upon his hands as he used to have, she did not make a light before him, his house was in darkness, and she was lying very sick. Her husband said to her, "Who has spoken with thee?"

Behold she said, "No one has spoken with me except thy younger brother. When he came to take for thee corn he found me sitting alone; he said to me, 'Come, let us stay together, tie up thy hair:' thus spake he to me. I did not listen to him, but thus spake I to him: 'Behold, am I not thy mother, is not thy elder brother to thee as a father?' And he feared, and he beat me to stop me from making report to thee, and if thou lettest him live I shall die. Now behold he is coming in the evening; and I complain of these wicked words, for he would have done this even in daylight."

And the elder brother became as a panther of the south; he sharpened his knife; he took it in his hand; he stood behind the door of his stable to slay his younger brother as he came in the evening to bring his cattle into the stable.

Now the sun went down, and he loaded himself with herbs in his daily manner. He came, and his foremost cow entered the stable, and she said to her keeper, "Behold thou thy elder brother standing before thee with his knife to slay thee; flee from before him." He heard what his first cow had said; and the next entering, she also said likewise. He looked beneath the door of the stable; he saw the feet of his elder brother; he was standing behind the door, and his knife was in his hand. He cast down his load to the ground, and betook himself to flee swiftly; and his elder brother pursued after him with his knife. Then the younger brother cried out unto Ra Harakhti, saying, "My good Lord! Thou art he who divides the evil from the good." And Ra stood and heard all his cry; and Ra made a wide water between him and his elder brother, and it was full of crocodiles; and the one brother was on one bank, and the other on the other bank; and the elder brother smote twice on his hands at not slaying him. Thus did he. And the younger brother called to the elder on the bank, saying, "Stand still until the dawn of day; and when Ra ariseth, I shall judge with thee before Him, and He discerneth between the good and the evil. For I shall not be with thee any more for ever; I shall not be in the place in which thou art; I shall go to the valley of the acacia."

Now when the land was lightened, and the next day appeared, Ra Harakhti arose, and one looked unto the other. And the youth spake with his elder brother, saying, "Wherefore earnest thou after me to slay me in craftiness, when thou didst not hear the words of my mouth? For I am thy brother in truth, and thou art to me as a father, and thy wife even as a mother: is it not so? Verily, when I was sent to bring for us corn, thy wife said to me, 'Come, stay with me;' for behold this has been turned over unto thee into another wise." And he caused him to understand of all that happened with him and his wife. And he swore an oath by Ra Har-akhti, saying, "Thy coming to slay me by deceit with thy knife was an abomination." Then the youth took a knife, and cut off of his flesh, and cast it into the water, and the fish swallowed it. He failed; he became

faint; and his elder brother cursed his own heart greatly; he stood weeping for him afar off; he knew not how to pass over to where his younger brother was, because of the crocodiles. And the younger brother called unto him, saying, "Whereas thou hast devised an evil thing, wilt thou not also devise a good thing, even like that which I would do unto thee? When thou goest to thy house thou must look to thy cattle, for I shall not stay in the place where thou art; I am going to the valley of the acacia. And now as to what thou shalt do for me; it is even that thou shalt come to seek after me, if thou perceivest a matter, namely, that there are things happening unto me. And this is what shall come to pass, that I shall draw out my soul, and I shall put it upon the top of the flowers of the acacia, and when the acacia is cut down, and it falls to the ground, and thou comest to seek for it, if thou searchest for it seven years do not let thy heart be wearied. For thou wilt find it, and thou must put it in a cup of cold water, and expect that I shall live again, that I may make answer to what has been done wrong.. And thou shalt know of this, that is to say, that things are happening to me, when one shall give to thee a cup of beer in thy hand, and it shall be troubled; stay not then, for verily it shall come to pass with thee."

And the youth went to the valley of the acacia; and his elder brother went unto his house; his hand was laid on his head, and he cast dust on his head; he came to his house, and he slew his wife, he cast her to the dogs, and he sat in mourning for his younger brother.

Now many days after these things, the younger brother was in the valley of the acacia; there was none with him; he spent his time in hunting the beasts of the desert, and he came back in the even to lie down under the acacia, which bore his soul upon the topmost flower.

And after this he built himself a tower with his own hands, in the valley of the acacia; it was full of all good things, that he might provide for himself a home.

And he went out from his tower, and he met the Nine Gods, who were walking forth to look upon the whole land. The Nine Gods talked one with another, and they said unto him, "Ho! Bata, bull of the Nine Gods, art thou remaining alone? Thou hast left thy village for the wife of Anpu, thy elder brother. Behold his wife is slain. Thou hast given him an answer to all that was transgressed against thee." And their hearts were vexed for him exceedingly. And Ra Harakhti said to Khnumu, "Behold, frame thou a woman for Bata, that he may not remain alive alone." And Khnumu made for him a mate to dwell with him.

She was more beautiful in her limbs than any woman who is in the whole land. The essence of every god was in her. The seven Hathors came to see her: they said with one mouth, "She will die a sharp death."

And Bata loved her very exceedingly, and she dwelt in his house; he passed his time in hunting the beasts of the desert, and brought and laid them before her. He said, "Go not outside, lest the sea seize thee; for I cannot rescue thee from it, for I am a woman like thee; my soul is placed on the head of the flower of the acacia; and if another find it, I must fight with him." And he opened unto her his heart in all its nature.

Now after these things Bata went to hunt in his daily manner. And the young girl went to walk under the acacia which was by the side of her house. Then the sea saw her, and cast its waves up after her. She betook herself to flee from before it. She entered her house. And the sea called unto the acacia, saying, "Oh, would that I could seize her!" And the acacia brought a lock from her hair, and the sea carried it to Egypt, and dropped it in the place of the fullers of Pharaoh's linen. The smell of the lock of hair entered into the clothes of Pharaoh; and they were wroth with the fullers of Pharaoh, saying, "The smell of ointment is in the clothes of Pharaoh." And the people were rebuked every day, they knew not what they should do. And the chief fuller of Pharaoh walked by the bank, and his heart was very evil within him after the daily quarrel with

him. He stood still, he stood upon the sand opposite to the lock of hair, which was in the water, and he made one enter into the water and bring it to him; and there was found in it a smell, exceeding sweet. He took it to Pharaoh; and they brought the scribes and the wise men, and they said unto Pharaoh, "This lock of hair belongs to a daughter of Ra Harakhti: the essence of every god is in her, and it is a tribute to thee from another land. Let messengers go to

every strange land to seek her: and as for the messenger who shall go to the valley of the acacia, let many men go with him to bring her." Then said his majesty, "Excellent exceedingly is what has been said to us;" and they sent them. And many days after these things the people who were sent to strange lands came to give report unto the king: but there came not those who went to the valley of the acacia, for Bata had slain them, but let one of them return to give a report to the king. His majesty sent many men and soldiers, as well as horsemen, to bring her back. And there was a woman amongst them, and to her had been given in her hand beautiful ornaments of a woman. And the girl came back with her, and they rejoiced over her in the whole land.

And his majesty loved her exceedingly, and raised her to high estate; and he spake unto her that she should tell him concerning her husband. And she said, "Let the acacia be cut down, and let one chop it up." And they sent men and soldiers with their weapons to cut down the acacia; and they came to the acacia, and they cut the flower upon which was the soul of Bata, and he fell dead suddenly.

And when the next day came, and the earth was lightened, the acacia was cut down. And Anpu, the elder brother of Bata, entered his house, and washed his hands; and one gave him a cup of beer, and it became troubled; and one gave him another of wine, and the smell of it was evil. Then he took his staff, and his sandals, and likewise his clothes, with his weapons of war; and .he betook himself forth to the valley of the acacia. He entered the tower of his younger brother, and he found him lying upon his mat; he was dead. And he wept when he saw his younger brother verily lying dead. And he went out to seek the soul of his younger brother under the acacia tree, under which his younger brother lay in the evening.

He spent three years in seeking for it, but found it not. And when he began the fourth year, he desired in his heart to return into Egypt; he said "I will go to-morrow morn: " thus spake he in his heart.

Now when the land lightened, and the next day appeared, he was walking under the acacia; he was spending his time in seeking it. And he returned in the evening, and laboured at seeking it again. He found a seed. He returned with it. Behold this was the soul of his younger brother. He brought a cup of cold water, and he cast the seed into it: and he sat down, as he was wont. Now when the night came his soul sucked up the water; Bata shuddered in all his limbs, and he looked on his elder brother; his soul was in the cup. Then Anpu took the cup of cold water, in which the soul of his younger brother was; Bata drank it, his soul stood again in its place, and he became as he had been. They embraced each other, and they conversed together. And Bata said to his elder brother, "Behold I am to become as a great bull, which bears every good mark; no one knoweth its history, and thou must sit upon my back. When the sun arises I shall be in the place where my wife is, that I may return answer to her; and thou must take me to the place where the king is. For all good things shall be done for thee; for one shall lade thee with silver and gold, because thou bringest me to Pharaoh, for I become a great marvel, and they shall rejoice for me in all the land. And thou shalt go to thy village."

And when the land was lightened, and the next day appeared, Bata became in the form which he had told to his elder brother. And Anpu sat upon his back until the dawn. He came to the place where the

king was, and they made his majesty to know of him; he saw him, and he was exceeding joyful with him. He made for him great offerings, saying, "This is a great wonder which has come to pass." There were rejoicings over him in the whole land. They presented unto him silver and gold for his elder brother, who went and stayed in his village. They gave to the bull many men and many things, and Pharaoh loved him exceedingly above all that is in this land.

And after many days after these things, the bull entered the purified place; he stood in the place where the princess was; he began to speak with her, saying, "Behold, I am alive indeed." And she said to him, "And, pray, who art thou?" He said to her, "I am Bata. I perceived when thou causedst that they should destroy the acacia of Pharaoh, which was my abode, that I might not be suffered to live. Behold, I am alive indeed, I am as an ox." Then the princess feared exceedingly for the words that her husband had spoken to her. And he went out from the purified place.

And his majesty was sitting, making a good day with her: she was at the table of his majesty, and the king was exceeding pleased with her. And she said to his majesty, "Swear to me by God, saying, 'What thou shalt say, I will obey it for thy sake.'" He hearkened unto all that she said, even this. "Let me eat of the liver of the ox, because he is fit for nought:" thus spake she to him. And the king was exceeding sad at her words, the heart of Pharaoh grieved him greatly. And after the land was lightened, and the next day appeared, they proclaimed a great feast with offerings to the ox. And the king sent one of the chief butchers of his majesty, to cause the ox to be sacrificed. And when he was sacrificed, as he was upon the shoulders of the people, he shook his neck, and he threw two drops of blood over against the two doors of his majesty. The one fell upon the one side, on the great door of Pharaoh, and the other upon the other door. They grew as two great Persea trees, and each of them was excellent.

And one went to tell unto his majesty, "Two great Persea trees have grown, as a great marvel of his majesty, in the night by the side of the great gate of his majesty." And there was rejoicing for them in all the land, and there were offerings made to them.

And when the days were multiplied after these things, his majesty was adorned with the blue crown, with garlands of flowers on his neck, and he was upon the chariot of pale gold, and he went out from the palace to behold the Persea trees: the princess also was going out with horses behind his majesty. And his majesty sat beneath one of the Persea trees, and it spake thus with his wife: "Oh thou deceitful one, I am Bata, I am alive, though I have been evilly entreated. I knew who caused the acacia to be cut down by Pharaoh at my dwelling. I then became an ox, and thou causedst that I should be killed."

And many days after these things the princess stood at the table of Pharaoh, and the king was pleased with her. And she said to his majesty, "Swear to me by God, saying, 'That which the princess shall say to me I will obey it for her.'" And he hearkened unto all she said.

And he commanded, "Let these two Persea trees be cut down, and let them be made into goodly planks." And he hearkened unto all she said. And after this his majesty sent skilful craftsmen, and they cut down the Persea trees of Pharaoh; and the princess, the royal wife, was standing looking on, and they did all that was in her heart unto the trees. But a chip flew up, and it entered into the mouth of the princess; she swallowed it, and after many days she bore a son. And one went to tell his majesty, "There is born to thee a son." And they brought him, and gave to him a nurse and servants; and there were rejoicings in the whole land. And the king sat making a merry day, as they were about the naming of him, and his majesty loved him exceedingly at that moment, and the king raised him to be the royal son of Kush.

Now after the days had multiplied after these things, his majesty made him heir of all the land. And many days after that, when he had fulfilled many years as heir, his majesty flew up to heaven. And the heir said, "Let my great nobles of his majesty be brought before me, that I may make them to know all that has happened to me." And they brought also before him his wife, and he judged with her before him, and they agreed with him. They brought to him his elder brother; he made him hereditary prince in all his land. He was thirty years king of Egypt, and he died, and his elder brother stood in his place on the day of burial.

Excellently finished in peace, for the ka of the scribe of the treasury Kagabu, of the treasury of Pharaoh, and for the scribe Hora, and the scribe Meremapt. Written by the scribe Anena, the owner of this roll. He who speaks against this roll, may Tahuti smite him.

REMARKS

This tale, which is perhaps, of all this series, the best known in modern times, has often been published. It exists only in one papyrus, that of Madame d'Orbiney, purchased by the British Museum in 1857. The papyrus had belonged to Sety II. when crown prince, and hence is of the XlXth Dynasty. Most of the great scholars of this age have worked at it: De Rouge, Goodwin, Renouf, Chabas, Brugsch, Ebers, Maspero, and Groff have all made original studies on it. The present translation is, however, a fresh one made by Mr. Griffith word for word, and shaped as little as possible by myself in editing it. The copy followed is the publication by Birch in "Select Papyri," part ii. pls. ix. to xix. Before considering the details of the story, we should notice an important question about its age and composition. That it is as old as the XIXth Dynasty in its present form is certain from the papyrus; but probably parts of it are older. The idyllic beauty of the opening of it, with the simplicity and directness of the ideas, and the absence of any impossible or marvellous feature, is in the strongest opposition to the latter part, where marvel is piled on marvel in pointless profusion. In the first few pages there is not a word superfluous or an idea out of place in drawing the picture. That we have to do with an older story lengthened out by some inartistic compiler, seems only too probable. And this is borne out by the colophon. In the tales of the Shipwrecked Sailor, and of Sanehat, the colophon runs--"This is finished from beginning to end, even as it was found in the writing," and the earlier of these two tales follows this with a blessing on the transcriber. But, apparently conscious of his meddling, the author of Anpu and Bata ends with a curse: "Written by the scribe Anena, the owner of this roll. He who speaks against this roll, may Tahuti smite him."

This points to a part of it at least being newly composed in Ramesside times; while the delicate beauty of the opening is not only far better than the latter part, but is out of harmony with the forced and artificial taste of the XIXth Dynasty. At the same time, the careful drawing of character is hardly akin to the simple, matter-of-fact style of Sanehat, and seems more in keeping with the emotional style of the Doomed Prince. If we attribute the earlier part to the opening of the XVIIIth Dynasty--the age of the pastoral scenes of the tombs of El Kab, which are the latest instances of such sculptures in Egypt--we shall probably be nearest to the truth.

The description of Bata is one of the most beautiful character-drawings in the past. The self-denial and sweet innocence of the lad, his sympathy with his cattle, "listening to all that they said," and allowing them their natural wishes and ways, is touchingly expressed. And those who know Egypt will know that Bata still lives there--several Batas I have known myself. His sweetness of manner, his devotion, his untiringly earnest work, his modesty, his quietness, makes Bata to be one of the most charming friends. Bata I have met in many places, Bata I have loved as one of the flowers of human nature, and Bata I hope often to meet again in divers forms and varied incarnations among the fellah lads of Egypt.

The touches of description of Bata are slight, and yet so pointed. His growing to be an excellent worker; his return at evening laden with all the produce, just as may be seen now any evening as the lads come in bearing on their backs large bundles of vegetables for the house, and of fodder for the home-driven cattle; his sleeping with his cattle in the stable; his zeal in rising before dawn to make the daily bread for his brother, ready to give him when he arose; and then his driving out the cattle to pasture--all contrasts with his elder brother's life of ease. The making of the bread was rightly the duty of Anpu's wife; she ought to have risen to grind the corn long before dawn, as the millstones may now be heard grinding in the dark, morning by morning; she ought to have baked the bread ready for the toiler who spent his whole day in the field. But it was the ever-willing Bata who did the work of the house as well as the work of the farm. "Behold the spirit of a god was in him."

The driving in of the cattle at night is still a particular feature of Egyptian life. About an hour before sunset the tether ropes are drawn in the fields, and the cattle file off, with a little child for a leader--if any; the master gathers up the produce that is required, some buffalo is laden with a heap of clover, or a lad carries it on his back, for the evening feed of the cattle, and all troop along the path through the fields and by the canal. For two or three miles the road becomes more and more crowded with the flocks driven into it from every field, a long haze of dust lies glowing in the crimson glory of sunset over the stream of cows and buffaloes, sheep and goats, that pour into the village. Each beast well knows his master and his crib, and turns in at the familiar gate to the stable under the house, or by the side of the hut; and there all spend the night. Not a hoof is left out in the field; the last belated stragglers come in while the gleam of amber still edges the night-blue sky behind the black horizon. Then the silent fields lie under the brightening moon, glittering with dew, untrodden and deserted. It is not cold or climate that leads men to this custom, but the unsafety of a country bordered by unseen deserts, whence untold men may suddenly appear and ravage all the plain.

The ploughing scene next follows, on "the land coming out from the water"; as the inundation goes down the well-known banks and ridges appear, "the back-bones of the land," as they were so naturally called; and when the surface is firm enough to walk on--with many a pool and ditch still full--the ploughing begins on the soft dark clay

The catastrophe of the story--the black gulf of deceit that suddenly opens under Bata's feet--has always been seen to be strikingly like the story of Joseph. And--as we have noticed--there is good reason for the early part of this tale belonging to about the beginning of the XVIIIth Dynasty, so it is very closely allied in time as well as character to the account of Joseph. In this part again is one of those pointed touches, which show the power of the poet--for a poem in prose this is--"her heart knew him with the knowledge of youth."

On reaching the mistaken revenge of Anpu, we see the sympathy of Bata with his cattle, and his way of reading their feelings, returned to him most fittingly by the cows perceiving the presence of the treachery. "He heard what his first cow had said; and the next entering she also said likewise."

After this we find a change; instead of the simple and natural narrative, full of human feeling, and without a touch of impossibility, every subsequent episode involves the supernatural; Ra creating a wide water, the extraction of the soul of Bata, his miraculous wife, and all the transformations--these have nothing in common with the style or ideas of the earlier tale.

Whence this later tangle came, and how much of it is drawn from other sources, we can hardly hope to explain from the fragments of literature that we have. But strangely there is a parallel which is close enough to suggest that the patchwork is due to popular mythology. In the myths of Phrygia we meet with Atys or Attis, of whom varying legends are told. Among these we glean that he was a shepherd, beautiful and chaste; that he fled from corruption; that he mutilated himself; lastly he died under a tree, and afterwards was revived. All this is a duplicate of the story of Bata. And looking further, we see parallels to the three subsequent transformations. Drops of blood were shed from the Atys-priest; and Bata, in his first transformation as a bull, sprinkles two drops of blood by the doors of the palace. Again, Atys is identified with a tree, which was cut down and taken into a sanctuary; and Bata in his second transformation is a Persea tree which is cut down and used in building. Lastly, the mother of Atys is said to have been a virgin, who bore him from placing in her bosom a ripe almond or pomegranate; and in his third transformation Bata is born from a chip of a tree being swallowed by the princess. These resemblances in nearly all the main points are too close and continuous to be a mere chance, especially as such incidents are not found in any other Egyptian tale, nor in few--if any--other classical myths. It is not impossible that the names even may have been the same; for Bata, as we write it, was pronounced Vata (or Vatiu or Vitiou, as others would vocalise it), and the digamma would disappear in the later Greek form in which we have Atys.

The most likely course seems to have been that, starting with a simple Egyptian tale, the resemblance to the shepherd of the Asiatic myth, led to a Ramesside author improving the story by tacking on the branches of the myth one after another, and borrowing the name. If this be granted, we have here in Bata the earliest indications of the elements of the Atys mysteries, a thousand years before the Greek versions.

Returning now from the general structure to the separate incidents, we note the expression of annoyance where the elder brother "smote twice on his hands." This gesture is very common in Egypt now, the two hands being rapidly slid one past the other, palm to palm, vertically, grating the fingers of one hand over the other; the right hand moving downwards, and the left a little up. This implies that there is nothing, that a thing is worthless, that a desired result has not been attained, or annoyance at want of success; but the latter meanings are now rare, and more latent than otherwise, and this tale points to the gesture being originally one of positive anger, though it has been transferred gradually to express mere negative results.

The valley of the acacia would appear from the indications to have been by the sea, and probably in Syria; perhaps one of the half-desert wadis toward Gaza was in the writer's mind. The idea of Bata taking out his heart, and placing it on the flower of a tree, has seemed hopelessly unintelligible. But it depends on what we are to understand by the heart in Egyptian. Two words are well known for it, hati and ah; and as it is unlikely that these should be mere synonyms, we have a presumption that one of them does not mean the physical heart, but rather the mental heart. We are accustomed to the same mixture of thought; and far the more common usage in English is not to employ the name to express the physical heart, but for the will, as when we say "good-hearted";--for the spring of action, "broken-hearted ";--for the feelings, "hard-hearted";--for the passions, "an affair of the heart";--or for the vigour, as when a man in nature or in act is "hearty" The Egyptian, with his metaphysical mind, took two different words where we only use one; and when we read of placing the heart (hati) out of a man, we are led at once by the analogy of beliefs in other races to understand this as the vitality or soul. In the "Golden Bough" Mr. Frazer has explained this part of natural metaphysics; and in this, and the following points, I freely quote from that work as a convenient text-book. The soul or vitality of a man is thought of as separable from the body at will, and therefore communicable to other objects or positions. In those positions it cannot be harmed by what happens to the body, which is therefore deathless for the time. But if the external seat of the soul be attacked or destroyed, the man immediately dies. This is illustrated from the Norse, Saxons, Celts, Italians, Greeks, Kabyles, Arabs, Hindus, Malays, Mongolians, Tartars, Magyars, and Slavonians. It may well, then, be considered as a piece of inherent psychology: and following this interpretation, I have rendered "heart" in this sense "soul" in the translation.

The Nine Gods who meet Bata are one of the great cycles of divinities, which were differently reckoned in various places. Khnumu is always the formative god, who makes man upon the potter's wheel, as in the scene in the temple of Luqsor. And even in natural birth it was Khnumu who "gave strength to the limbs," as in the earlier "Tales of the Magicians." The character of the wife of Bata is a very curious study. The total absence of the affections in her was probably designed as in accord with her non-natural formation, as she could not inherit aught from human parents. Ambition appears as the only emotion of this being; her attacks on the transformations of Bata are not due to dislike, but only to fear that he should claim her removal from her high station; she "feared exceedingly for the words that her husband had spoken to her." Her Lilith nature is incapable of any craving but that for power.

The action here of the seven Hathors we have noticed in the remarks on the previous tale of the Doomed Prince. The episode of the sea is very strange; and if we need find some rationalising account of it, we might suppose it to be a mythical form of a raid of pirates, who, not catching the woman, carried off something of hers, which proved an object of contention in Egypt. But such renderings are unlikely, and we may the rather expect to find some explanation in a mythological parallel.

The carrying of the lock of hair to Pharaoh, and his proclaiming a search for the owner, is plainly an early form of the story of the little slipper, whose owner is sought by the king. The point that she could not be caught except by setting another woman to tempt her with ornaments, anticipates the modern novelist's saying, "Set a woman to catch a woman."

The sudden death of Bata, so soon as the depository of his soul was destroyed, is a usual feature in such tales about souls. But it is only in the Indian forms quoted by Mr. Frazer that there is any revival of the dead; and in no case is there any transformation like that of Bata. Perhaps none but an Egyptian or a Chinese would have credited Anpu with wandering up and down for four years seeking the lost soul. But the idea of returning the soul in water to the man is found as a magic process in North America ("Golden Bough," i. 141).

The first transformation of Bata, into a bull, is clearly drawn from the Apis bull of Memphis. The rejoicings at discovering a real successor of Apis are here, the rejoicings over Bata, who is the Apis bull, distinguished as he says by "bearing every good mark." These marks on the back and other parts were the tokens of the true Apis, who was sought for anxiously through the country on the death of the sacred animal who had lived in the sanctuary. The man who, like Anpu, brought up a true Apis to the temple would receive great rewards and honours.

The scene where the princess demands the grant of a favour is repeated over again by Esther at her banquet, and by the daughter of Herodias. It is the Oriental way of doing business. But the curious incongruity of making a great feast with offerings to the ox before sacrificing it, appears inexplicable until we note the habits of other peoples in slaying their sacred animals at certain intervals. This tale shows us what is stated by Greek authors, that the Egyptians slew the sacred Apis at stated times, or when a new one was discovered with the right marks. The annual sacrifice of a sacred ram at Thebes shows that the

Egyptians were familiar with such an idea. And though it was considered by the writer of this tale as a monstrous act, yet the offerings and festivity which accompanied it are in accordance with the strange fact found by Mariette, that in the three undisturbed Apis burials which he discovered there were only fragments of bone, and in one case a head, carefully embalmed with bitumen and magnificent offerings of jewellery. The divine Apis was eaten as a sacred feast.

The reason that the princess desires the liver is strangely explained by a present belief on the Upper Nile. The Darfuris think that the liver is the seat of the soul ("Golden Bough," ii. 88); and hence if she ate the liver she would destroy the soul of Bata, or prevent it entering any other incarnation.

The next detail is also curiously significant. If a bull was being sacrificed we should naturally suppose the blood would flow, and that a few drops would not be noticed. Here, however, two drops are said to fall, and this was when the bull "was upon the shoulders of the people." Now it is a very general idea that blood must not be allowed to fall upon the ground; the eastern and southern Africans will not shed the blood of cattle ("Golden Bough," i. 182); and strangely the Australians avoid the falling of blood to the ground by placing the bleeding persons upon the shoulders of other men. This parallel is so close to the Egyptian tale that it seems as if the bull was borne "on the shoulders of the people," that his blood should not fall to the ground; yet in spite of this precaution "he shook his neck, and he threw two drops of blood over against the doors of his majesty." In these drops of blood was the soul of Bata, in spite of the princess having eaten his liver; and we know how among Jews, Arabs, and other peoples, the blood is regarded as the vehicle of the soul or life.

The evidence of tree worship is plainer here than perhaps in any other passage of Egyptian literature. The people rejoice for the two Persea trees, "and there were offerings made to them."

The blue crown worn by the king was the war cap of leather covered with scales of copper: it is often found made in dark blue glaze for statuettes, and it seems probable that the copper was superficially sulphurised to tint it. Such head-dress was usually worn by kings when riding in their chariots. The pale gold or electrum here mentioned was the general material for decorating the royal chariot.

The miraculous birth of Bata in his third transformation is, as we have noticed, closely paralleled by the birth of Atys from the almond. The idea at the root of this is that of self-creation or self-existence, as in the usual Egyptian phrase, "bull of his mother."

The king flying up to heaven is a regular expression for his death: "the hawk has soared," "the follower of the god has met his maker," so Sanehat describes it (see ist series, pp. 97, 98).

This hawk-form of the king may be connected with the hawk bearing the double crown which is perched on the top of the ka name of each king. That hawk is not Horus, nor even the king deified as Horus, because the emblem of life is given to it by other gods (as by Set on a lintel of XVIIIth Dynasty from Nubt), and therefore the hawk is the human king who could perish, and not an immortal divinity. Further, this hawk-king is always perched on the top of the drawing of the doorway to the sepulcher which bears the ka name of the king; and when we see the drawings of the ba bird or soul flying down the well to the sepulchre, it appears as if the hawk were the royal ba bird (ordinary men having a ba bird with a human head); and that the well-known first title of each

149

king represents the royal soul or ba bird perched on the door of the sepulchre, resting on his way to and from the visit to the corpse below. The soul or ba of the king at his death thus flew away as a hawk to meet the sun.

The veil drawn over the fate of the inhuman princess is well conceived. That she should die a sharp death has been foretold; but how Bata should slay the divine creation--his wife--his mother--is a matter that the scribe reserves in silence; we only read that "he judged with her before him, and the great nobles agreed with him." That judgment is best left among the things unwritten, The strange manner in which we can see incident after incident in the latter part of the tale, each to refer to some ceremony or belief, even imperfect as our knowledge of such must be, and the evidence that the whole being of Bata is a transference of the myth of Atys, must lead us to look on this, the marvellous portion, as woven out of a group of myths, ceremonies, and beliefs which were joined and explained by the formation of such a tale. How far it is due to purely Egyptian ideas, indicated by the Apis bull and the analogies in present African beliefs, and how far it is Asiatic and belonging to Atys, it would be premature to decide. But from the weird confusion and mystery of these transformations, we turn back with renewed pleasure to the simple and sweet picture of peasant life, and the beauty of Bata, and we see how true a poet the Egyptian was in feeling and in expression.

XIXth DYNASTY, PTOLEMAIC WRITING

SETNA AND THE MAGIC BOOK

THE mighty King User.maat.ra (Ra-meses the Great) had a son named Setna Kha.em.uast who was a great scribe, and very learned in all the ancient writings. And he heard that the magic book of Thoth, by which a man may enchant heaven and earth, and know the language of all birds and beasts, was buried in the cemetery of Memphis. And he went to search for it with his brother An.he.hor.eru; and when they found the tomb of the king's son, Na.nefer.ka.ptah, son of the king of Upper and Lower Egypt, Mer.neb.ptah, Setna opened it and went in.

Now in the tomb was Na.nefer.ka.ptah, and with him was the ka of his wife Ahura; for though she was buried at Koptos, her ka dwelt at Memphis with her husband, whom she loved. And Setna saw them seated before their offerings, and the book lay between them. And Na.nefer.ka.ptah said to Setna, "Who are you that break into my tomb in this way?" He said,

"I am Setna, son of the great King User.maat.ra, living for ever, and I come for that book which I see between you." And Na.nefer.ka.ptah said, "It cannot be given to you." Then said Setna, "But I will carry it away by force."

Then Ahura said to Setna, "Do not take this book; for it will bring trouble on you, as it has upon us. Listen to what we have suffered for it."

"We were the two children of the King Mer.neb.ptah, and he loved us very much, for he had no others; and Na.nefer.ka.ptah was in his palace as heir over all the land. And when we were grown, the king said to the queen, 'I will marry Na.nefer.ka.ptah to the daughter of a general, and Ahura to the son of another general.' And the queen said, 'No, he is the heir, let him marry his sister, like the heir of a king, none other is fit for him.' And the king said, 'That is not fair; they had better be married to the children of the general.'

"And the queen said, 'It is you who are not dealing rightly with me.' And the king answered, 'If I have no more than these two children, is it right that they should marry one another? I will marry Na.nefer.ka.ptah to the daughter of an officer, and Ahura to the son of another officer. It has often been done so in our family.'

"And at a time when there was a great feast before the king, they came to fetch me to the feast. And I was very troubled, and did not behave as I used to do. And the king said to me, 'Ahura, have you sent some one to me about this sorry matter, saying, "Let me be married to my elder brother"'? 'I said to him, 'Well, let me marry the son of an officer, and he marry the daughter of another officer, as it often happens so in our family.' I laughed, and the king laughed. And the king told the steward of the palace, 'Let them take Ahura to the house of Na.nefer.ka.ptah to-night, and all kinds of good things with her.' So they brought me as a wife to the house of Na.nefer.ka.ptah; and the king ordered them to give me presents of silver and gold, and things from the palace.

"And Na.nefer.ka.ptah passed a happy time with me, and received all the presents from the palace; and we loved one another. And when I expected a child, they told the king, and he was most heartily glad; and he sent me many things, and a present of the best silver and gold and linen. And when the time came, I bore this little child that is before you. And they gave him the name of Mer-ab, and registered him in the book of the 'House of life.'

"And when my brother Na.nefer.ka.ptah went to the cemetery of Memphis, he did nothing on earth but read the writings that are in the catacombs of the kings, and the tablets of the 'House of life,' and the

inscriptions that are seen on the monuments, and he worked hard on the writings. And there was a priest there called Nesi-ptah; and as Na.nefer.ka.ptah went into a temple to pray, it happened that he went behind this priest, and was reading the inscriptions that were on the chapels of the gods. And the priest mocked him and laughed. So Na.nefer.ka.ptah said to him, 'Why are you laughing at me?' And he replied, 'I was not laughing at you, or if I happened to do so, it was at your reading writings that are worthless. If you wish so much to read writings, come to me, and I will bring you to the place where the book is which Thoth himself wrote with his own hand, and which will bring you to the gods. When you read but two pages in this you will enchant the heaven, the earth, the abyss, the mountains, and the sea; you shall know what the birds of the sky and the crawling things are saying; you shall see the fishes of the deep, for a divine power is there to bring them up out of the depth. And when you read the second page, if you are in the world of ghosts, you will become again in the shape you were in on earth. You will see the sun shining in the sky, with all the gods, and the full moon.'

"And Na.nefer.ka.ptah said, 'By the life of the king! Tell me of anything you want done and I'll do it for you, if you will only send me where this book is.' And the priest answered Na.nefer.ka.ptah, 'If you want to go to the place where the book is, you must give me a hundred pieces of silver for my funeral, and provide that they shall bury me as a rich priest.' So Na.nefer.ka.ptah called his lad and told him to give the priest a hundred pieces of silver; and he made them do as he wished, even everything that he asked for. Then the priest said to Na.nefer.ka.ptah, 'This book is in the middle of the river at Koptos, in an iron box; in the iron box is a bronze box; in the bronze box is a sycamore box; in the sycamore box is an ivory and ebony box; in the ivory and ebony box is a silver box; in the silver box is a golden box, and in that is the book. It is twisted all round with snakes and scorpions and all the other crawling things around the box in which the book is; and there is a deathless snake by the box.' And when the priest told Na.nefer.ka.ptah, he did not know where on earth he was, he was so much delighted.

"And when he came from the temple he told me all that had happened to him. And he said, 'I shall go to Koptos, for I must fetch this book; I will not stay any longer in the north.' And I said, 'Let me dissuade you, for you prepare sorrow and you will bring me into trouble in the Thebaid.' And I laid my hand on Na.nefer.ka.ptah, to keep him from going to Koptos, but he would not listen to me; and he went to the king, and told the king all that the priest had said. The king asked him, 'What is it that you want?' and he replied, 'Let them give me the royal boat with its belongings, for I will go to the south with Ahura and her little boy Mer-ab, and fetch this book without delay.' So they gave him the royal boat with its belongings, and we went with him to the haven, and sailed from there up to Koptos.

"Then the priests of Isis of Koptos, and the high priest of Isis, came down to us without waiting, to meet Na.nefer.ka.ptah, and their wives also came to me. We went into the temple of Isis and Harpokrates; and Na.nefer.ka.ptah brought an ox, a goose, and some wine, and made a burnt-offering and a drink-offering before Isis of Koptos and Harpokrates. They brought us to a very fine house, with all good things; and Na.nefer.ka.ptah spent four days there and feasted with the priests of Isis of Koptos, and the wives of the priests of Isis also made holiday with me. "And the morning of the fifth day came; and Na.nefer.ka.ptah called a priest to him, and made a magic cabin that was full of men and tackle. He put the spell upon it, and put life in it, and gave them breath, and sank it in the water. He filled the royal boat with sand, and took leave of me, and sailed from the haven: and I sat by the river at Koptos that I might see what would become of him. And he said, 'Workmen, work for me, even at the place where the book is.' And they toiled by night and by day; and when they had reached it in three days, he threw the sand out, and made a shoal in the river. And then he found on it entwined serpents and scorpions and all kinds of crawling things around the box in which the book was; and by it he found a deathless snake around the box. And he laid the spell upon the entwined serpents and scorpions and all kinds of crawling things which were around the box, that they should not come out. And he went to the deathless snake, and fought with him, and killed him; but he came to life again, and took a new form. He then fought again with him a second time; but he came to life again, and took a third form. He then cut him in two parts, and put sand between the parts, that he should not appear again.

"Na.nefer.ka.ptah then went to the place where he found the box. He uncovered a box of iron, and opened it; he found then a box of bronze, and opened that; then he found a box of sycamore wood, and opened that; again, he found a box of ivory and ebony, and opened that; yet, he found a box of silver, and opened that; and then he found a box of gold; he opened that, and found the book in it. He took the book from the golden box, and read a page of spells from it. He enchanted the heaven and the earth, the abyss, the mountains, and the sea; he knew what the birds of the sky, the fish of the deep, and the beasts of the hills all said. He read another page of the spells, and saw the sun shining in the sky, with all the gods, the full moon, and the stars in their shapes; he saw the fishes of the deep, for a divine power was present that brought them up from the water. He then read the spell upon the workmen that he had made, and taken from the haven, and said to them, 'Work for me, back to the place from which I came.' And they toiled night and day, and so he came back to the place where I sat by the river of Koptos; I had not drunk nor eaten anything, and had done nothing on earth, but sat like one who is gone to the grave.

"I then told Na.nefer.ka.ptah that I wished to see this book, for which we had taken so much trouble. He gave the book into my hands; and when I read a page of the spells in it I also enchanted heaven and earth, the abyss, the mountains, and the sea; I also knew what the birds of the sky, the fishes of the deep, and the beasts of the hills all said. I read another page of the spells, and I saw the sun shining in the sky with all the gods, the full moon, and the stars in their shapes; I saw the fishes of the deep, for a divine power was present that brought them up from the water. As I could not write, I asked Na.nefer.ka.ptah, who was a good writer, and a very learned one; he called for a new piece of papyrus, and wrote on it all that was in the book before him. He dipped it in beer, and washed it off in the liquid; for he knew that if it were washed off, and he drank it, he would know all that there was in the writing.

"We returned back to Koptos the same day, and made a feast before Isis of Koptos and Harpokrates. We then went to the haven and sailed, and went northward of Koptos. And as we went on Thoth discovered all that Na.nefer.ka.ptah had done with the book; and Thoth hastened to tell Ra, and said, 'Now know that my book and my revelation are with Na.nefer.ka.ptah, son of the King Mer.neb.ptah. He has forced himself into my place, and robbed it, and seized my box with the writings, and killed my guards who protected it.' And Ra replied to him, 'He is before you, take him and all his kin.' He sent a power from heaven with the command, 'Do not let Na.nefer.ka.ptah return safe to Memphis with all his kin.' And after this hour, the little boy Mer-ab, going out from the awning of the royal boat, fell into the river: he called on Ra, and everybody who was on the bank raised a cry. Na.nefer.ka.ptah went out of the cabin, and read the spell over him; he brought his body up because a divine power brought him to the surface. He read another spell over him, and made him tell of all what happened to him, and of what Thoth had said before Ra.

"We turned back with him to Koptos. We brought him to the Good House, we fetched the people to him, and made one embalm him; and we buried him in his coffin in the cemetery of Koptos like a great and noble person.

"And Na.nefer.ka.ptah, my brother, said, 'Let us go down, let us not delay, for the king has not yet heard of what has happened to him, and his heart will be sad about it.' So we went to the haven, we sailed, and did not stay to the north of Koptos. When we were come to the place where the little boy Mer-ab had fallen in the water, I went out from the awning of the royal boat, and I fell into the river. They called Na.nefer.ka.ptah, and he came out from the cabin of the royal boat; he read a spell over me, and brought my body up, because a divine power brought me to the surface. He drew me out, and read the spell over me, and made me tell him of all that had happened to me, and of what Thoth had said before Ra. Then he turned back with me to Koptos, he brought me to the Good House, he fetched the people to me, and made one embalm me, as great and noble people are buried, and laid me in the tomb where Mer-ab my young child was. "He turned to the haven, and sailed down, and delayed not in the north of Koptos. When he was come to the place where we fell into the river, he said to his heart, 'Shall I not better turn back again to Koptos, that I may lie by them? For, if not, when I go down to Memphis, and the king asks after his children, what shall I say to him? Can I tell him, "I have

taken your children to the Thebaid, and killed them, while I remained alive, and I have come to Memphis still alive"?' Then he made them bring him a linen cloth of striped byssus; he made a band, and bound the book firmly, and tied it upon him. Na.nefer.ka.ptah then went out of the awning of the royal boat and fell into the river. He cried on Ra; and all those who were on the bank made an outcry, saying, 'Great woe! Sad woe! Is he lost, that good scribe and able man that has no equal?'

"The royal boat went on, without any one on earth knowing where Na.nefer.ka.ptah was. It went on to Memphis, and they told all this to the king. Then the king went down to the royal boat in mourning, and all the soldiers and high priests and priests of Ptah were in mourning, and all the officials and courtiers. And when he saw Na.nefer.ka.ptah, who was in the inner cabin of the royal boat--from his rank of high scribe--he lifted him up. And they saw the book by him; and the king said, 'Let one hide this book that is with him.' And the officers of the king, the priests of Ptah, and the high priest of Ptah, said to the king, 'Our Lord, may the king live as long as the sun! Na.nefer.ka.ptah was a good scribe, and a very skilful man.' And the king had him laid in his Good House to the sixteenth day, and then had him wrapped to the thirty-fifth day, and laid him out to the seventieth day, and then had him put in his grave in his resting-place.

"I have now told you the sorrow which has come upon us because of this book for which you ask, saying, 'Let it be given to me.' You have no claim to it; and, indeed, for the sake of it, we have given up our life on earth."

And Setna said to Ahura, "Give me the book which I see between you and Na.nefer.ka.ptah; for if you do not I will take it by force." Then Na.nefer.ka.ptah rose from his seat and said, "Are you Setna, to whom my wife has told of all these blows of fate, which you have not suffered? Can you take this book by your skill as a good scribe? If, indeed, you can play games with me, let us play a game, then, of 52 points." And Setna said, "I am ready," and the board and its pieces were put before him. And Na.nefer.ka.ptah won a game from Setna; and he put the spell upon him, and defended himself with the game board that was before him, and sunk him into the ground above his feet. He did the same at the second game, and won it from Setna, and sunk him into the ground to his waist.

He did the same at the third game, and made him sink into the ground up to his ears. Then Setna struck Na.nefer.ka.ptah a great blow with his hand. And Setna called his brother An.he.hor.eru and said to him, "Make haste and go up upon earth, and tell the king all that has happened to me, and bring me the talisman of my father Ptah, and my magic books."

And he hurried up upon earth, and told the king all that had happened to Setna. The king said, "Bring him the talisman of his father Ptah, and his magic books." And An.he.hor.eru hurried down into the tomb; he laid the talisman on Setna, and he sprang up again immediately. And then Setna reached out his hand for the book, and took it. Then--as Setna went out from the tomb--there went a Light before him, and Darkness behind him. And Ahura wept at him, and she said, "Glory to the King of Darkness! Hail to the King of Light! all power is gone from the tomb." But Na.nefer.ka.ptah said to Ahura, "Do not let your heart be sad; I will make him bring back this book, with a forked stick in his hand, and a fire-pan on his head." And Setna went out from the tomb, and it closed behind him as it was before.

Then Setna went to the king, and told him everything that had happened to him with the book. And the king said to Setna, "Take back the book to the grave of Na.nefer.ka.ptah, like a prudent man, or else he will make you bring it with a forked stick in your hand, and a fire-pan on your head." But Setna would not listen to him; and when Setna had unrolled the book he did nothing on earth but read it to everybody.

[Here follows a story of how Setna, walking in the court of the temple of Ptah, met Tabubua, a fascinating girl, daughter of a priest of Bast, of Ankhtaui; how she repelled his advances, until she had beguiled him into giving up all his possessions, and slaying his children. At the last she gives a fearful cry and vanishes, leaving Setna bereft of even his clothes. This would seem to be merely a dream, by the disappearance of Tabubua, and by Setna finding his children alive after it all; but on the other hand he comes to his senses in an unknown place, and is so terrified as to be quite ready to make restitution to Na.nefer.ka.ptah. The episode, which is not creditable to Egyptian society, seems

166

to be intended for one of the vivid dreams which the credulous readily accept as half realities.]

So Setna went to Memphis, and embraced his children for that they were alive. And the king said to him, "Were you not drunk to do so?" Then Setna told all things that had happened with Tabubua and Na.nefer. ka.ptah. And the king said, "Setna, I have already lifted up my hand against you before, and said, 'He will kill you if you do not take back the book to the place you took it from.' But you have never listened to me till this hour. Now, then, take the book to Na.nefer.ka.ptah, with a forked stick in your hand, and a fire-pan on your head."

So Setna went out from before the king, with a forked stick in his hand, and a firepan on his head. He went down to the tomb in which was Na.nefer.ka.ptah. And Ahura said to him, "It is Ptah, the great god, that has brought you back safe." Na.nefer.ka.ptah laughed, and he said, "This is the business that I told you before." And when Setna had praised Na.nefer.ka.ptah, he found it as the proverb says, "The sun was in the whole tomb." And Ahura and Na.nefer.ka.ptah besought Setna greatly. And Setna said, "Na.nefer.ka.ptah, is it aught disgraceful (that you lay on me to do)?" And Na.nefer.ka.ptah said, "Setna, you know this, that Ahura and Mer-ab, her child, behold! they are in Koptos; bring them here into this tomb, by the skill of a good scribe. Let it be impressed upon you to take pains, and to go to Koptos to bring them here." Setna then went out from the tomb to the king, and told the king all that Na.nefer.ka.ptah had told him.

The king said, "Setna, go to Koptos and bring back Ahura and Mer-ab." He answered the king, "Let one give me the royal boat and its belongings." And they gave him the royal boat and its belongings, and he left the haven, and sailed without stopping till he came to Koptos.

And they made this known to the priests of Isis at Koptos and to the high priest of Isis; and behold they came down to him, and gave him their hand to the shore. He went up with them and entered into the temple of Isis of Koptos and of Harpo-krates. He ordered one to offer for him an ox, a goose, and some wine, and he made a burnt-offering and a drink-offering before Isis of Koptos and Harpokrates. He went to the cemetery of Koptos with the priests of Isis and the high priest of Isis. They dug about for three days and three nights, for they searched even in all the catacombs which were in the cemetery of Koptos; they turned over the steles of the scribes of the "double house of life," and read the inscriptions that they found on them. But they could not find the resting-place of Ahura and Mer-ab.

Now Na.nefer.ka.ptah perceived that they could not find the resting-place of Ahura and her child Mer-ab. So he raised himself up as a venerable, very old, ancient, and came before Setna. And Setna saw him, and Setna said to the ancient, "You look like a very old man, do you know where is the resting-place of Ahura and her child Mer-ab?" The ancient said to Setna, "It was told by the father of the father of my father to the father of my father, and the father of my father has told it to my father; the resting-place of Ahura and of her child Mer-ab is in a mound south of the town of Pehemato (?)" And Setna said to the ancient, "Perhaps we may do damage to Pehemato, and you are ready to lead one to the town for the sake of that." The ancient replied to Setna, "If one listens to me, shall he therefore destroy the town of Pehemato! If they do not find Ahura and her child

Mer-ab under the south corner of their town may I be disgraced." They attended to the ancient, and found the resting-place of Ahura and her child Mer-ab under the south corner of the town of Pehemato. Setna laid them in the royal boat to bring them as honoured persons, and restored the town of Pehemato as it originally was. And Na.nefer.ka.ptah made Setna to know that it was he who had come to Koptos, to enable them to find out where the resting-place was of Ahura and her child Mer-ab.

So Setna left the haven in the royal boat, and sailed without stopping, and reached Memphis with all the soldiers who were with him. And when they told the king he came down to the royal boat. He took them as honoured persons escorted to the catacombs, in which Na.nefer.ka.ptah was, and smoothed down the ground over them.

This is the completed writing of the tale of Setna Kha.em.uast, and Na.nefer.ka.-ptah, and his wife Ahura, and their Mid Mer-ab. It was written in the 35th year, the month Tybi.

REMARKS

This tale of Setna only exists in one copy, a demotic papyrus in the Ghizeh Museum. The demotic was published in facsimile by Mariette in 1871, among "Les Papyrus du Musee de

Boulaq; " and it has been translated by Brugsch, Revillout, Maspero, and Hess. The last version-- "Der Demotische Roman von Stne Ha-m-us, von J. J. Hess"--being a full study of the text with discussion and glossary, has been followed here; while the interpretation of Maspero has also been kept in view in the rendering of obscure passages.

Unhappily the opening of this tale is lost, and I have therefore restored it by a recital of the circumstances which are referred to in what remains. Nothing has been introduced which is not necessarily involved or stated in the existing text. The limit of this restoration is marked by]; the papyrus beginning with the words, "It is you who are not dealing rightly with me."

The construction is complicated by the mixture of times and persons; and we must remember that it was written in the Ptolemaic period concerning an age long past. It stood to the author much as Tennyson's "Harold" stands to us, referring to an historical age, without too strict a tie to facts and details. Five different acts, as we may call them, succeed one another. In the first act--which is entirely lost, and here only outlined--the circumstances which led Setna of the XIXth Dynasty to search for the magic book must have been related. In the second act Ahura recites the long history of herself and family, to deter Setna from his purpose. This act is a complete tale by itself, and belongs to a time some generations before Setna; it is here supposed to belong to the time of Amenhotep III., in the details of costume adopted for illustration. The third act is Setna's struggle as a rival magician to Na.nefer.ka.ptah, from which he finally comes off victorious by his brother's use of a talisman, and so secures possession of the coveted magic book. The fourth act--which I have here only summarised--shows how Na.nefer.ka.ptah resorts to a bewitchment of Setna by a sprite, by subjection to whom he loses his magic power. The fifth act shows Setna as subjected to Na.nefer.ka.ptah, and ordered by him to bring the bodies of his wife and child to Memphis into his tomb.

While, therefore, the sentimental climax of the tale--the restoration of the unity of the family in one tomb--belongs to persons of the XVIIIth Dynasty, the action of the tale is entirely of the XlXth Dynasty, for what happened in the XVIIIth Dynasty (second act) is all related in the XlXth. And the actual composition of it belongs to Ptolemaic times, not only on the evidence of the manuscript, but also of the language; this being certified by the importance of Isis and Horus at Koptos, which is essentially a late worship there.

Turning now to the details, we may note that the statement that Setna Kha.em.uast was a son of User.maat.ra (or Ramessu II.) occurs in the fourth act which is here only summarised. Among the sons of Ramessu historically known, the Prince Kha.em.uast (or "Glory-in-Thebes ") was the most important; he appears to have been the eldest son, exercising the highest offices during his father's life. That the succession fell on the thirteenth son, Mer.en.ptah, was doubtless due to the elder sons having died during the preternaturally long reign of Ramessu.

The other main personage here is Na.nefer.ka.ptah (or "Excellent is the ka of Ptah "), who is said to be the son of a King Mer.neb. ptah. No such name is known among historical kings; and it is probably a popular corruption or abbreviation. It was pronounced Minibptah, the r being dropped in early times. It would seem most like Mine-ptah or Mer.en.ptah, the son and successor of Ramessu II.; but as the date of Mer.neb.ptah is supposed to be some generations before that, such a supposition would involve a great confusion on the scribes' part. Another possibility is that it represents Amenhotep III., Neb.maat.ra.mer.ptah, pronounced as Nimurimiptah, which might be shortened to Neb. mer.ptah or Mer.neb.ptah. Such a time would well suit the tale, and that reign has been adopted here in fixing the style of the dress of Ahura and her family.

This tale shows how far the ka or double might wander from its body or tomb. Here Ahura and her child lie buried at Koptos, while her husband's tomb is at Memphis. But that does not separate them in death; her ka left her tomb and went down to Memphis to live with the ka of her husband in his tomb. Thus, when Setna forces the tomb of Na.nefer.ka.ptah, he finds Ahura seated by him with the precious magic roll between them and the child Mer-ab; and the voluble Ahura recounts all their history, and weeps when the roll is carried away by Setna. Yet all the time her body is at Koptos, and the penalty imposed on Setna is that of bringing her body to the tomb where her ka already was dwelling. If a ka could thus wander so many hundred miles from its body to gratify its affections, it would doubtless run some risks of starving, or having to put up with impure food;

or might even lose its way, and rather than intrude on the wrong tomb, have to roam as a vagabond ka. It was to guard against these misfortunes that a supply of formulas were provided for it, by which it should obtain a guarantee against such misfortunes--a kind of spiritual directory or guide to the unprotected; and such formulas, when once accepted as valid, were copied, repeated, enlarged, and added to, until they became the complex and elaborate work--The Book of the Dead, Perhaps nothing else gives such a view of the action of the ka as this tale of Setna.

There is here also an insight into the arrangement of marriages in Egypt. It does not seem that anything was determined about a marriage during childhood; it is only when the children are full-grown that a dispute arises between the king and queen as to their disposal. But the parents decide the whole question. It is, of course, well known that the Egyptians had no laws against consanguinity in marriages; on the contrary, it was with them, as with the Persians, essential for a king to marry in the royal family, and also usual for private persons to marry in their family. Even to the present day in Egypt, although sister-marriage has disappeared, yet it is the duty of a man to marry his first cousin or some one in the family. The very idea of relationship being any possible impediment to marriage was un-thought of by the Egyptian; his favourite concrete expression for a self-existent or self-created being--"husband of his mother "-- shows this unmistakably.

The objection made by the king to the marriage of Na.nefer.ka.ptah and Ahura turns on the point that he has only these two children, and hence, if they marry the children of the generals, there will be two families instead of only one to ensure future posterity. The queen, however, talks the king over on the matter. The cause of Ahura's being troubled at the feast is not certain, but the king evidently supposes that she has been pleading to be allowed to marry her beloved brother, and when taxed with it she only expresses her willingness to give way to his exogamic views. The brief sentence, "I laughed and the king laughed," seems to mean that she pleased and amused her father so that he gave way, and immediately told the steward to arrange for her marriage as she desired. I have here abbreviated a few needlessly precise details. We also learn, by the way, that there was a regular registry of births, in which Mer-ab was entered.

It appears that the court was considered to be at Memphis, and not at Thebes. This would not have been so arranged had this been written in the Ramesside times, but under the Ptolemies Memphis was the seat of the court--when not at Alexandria. The name of the priest, Nesi-ptah, also shows another anachronism. Such a name was not usual till some time after the XIXth Dynasty. Another touch of late times is in the antiquarian curiosity of Na.nefer.ka.ptah about ancient writings, "He did nothing on earth but read the writings that are in the catacombs of the kings, and the tablets of the House of Life." In the XIXth Dynasty there is no sign of interest in such records, but in the Renascence ancient things came into fashion, all the old titles were revived, the old style was copied, and very long genealogies were worked up and carved in the inscriptions. In such an age many a dilettante rich young man would amuse himself, as in this tale, with reading inscriptions and hunting up his family genealogy from the tombstones and the registers.

The firm belief in magic which underlies all this tale might perhaps be thought to be inappropriate to the enlightenment of Greek times. We have seen how in the earliest tales magic is a mainspring of the action, and it is at first sight surprising that its sway should last through so many thousands of years. But there may well have been a recrudescence of such beliefs, along with the revival of interest in the earlier history. The enormous spread and popularity of Gnosticism--the belief in the efficacy of words and formulas to control spirits and their actions--in the centuries immediately after this, shows how ingrained magic ideas were, and how ready to sprout up when the counterbalancing interests of the old mythology were gone, and their place taken by the intangible spirituality of Platonism and the early Christian atmosphere.

A most Egyptian turn is given where the priest bargains for a large payment for his funeral, and to be buried as a rich priest. The enclosing of the magic roll in a series of boxes has many parallels. In an Indian tale we read: "Round the tree are tigers and bears and scorpions and snakes; on the top of the tree is a very fat great snake; on his head is a little cage; in the cage is a bird; and my soul is in that bird" ("Golden Bough," ii. 300). In Celtic tales the series-idea also occurs. The soul of a giant is in an egg, the egg is in a dove, the dove is in a hare, the hare is in a wolf, and the wolf is in an iron chest at the bottom of the sea ("Golden Bough," ii. 314). The Tartars have stories of a golden casket containing the soul, inside a copper or silver casket ("Golden Bough," ii. 324). And the Arabs tell of a soul put in the crop of a sparrow, and the sparrow in a little box, and this in another small box, and this put into seven other boxes, and these in seven chests, and the chest in a coffer of marble ("Golden 10 Bough," ii. 318). The notion, therefore, of a series of boxes, one enclosing another, and the whole guarded by dangerous animals, is well known as an element in tales. The late date is here shown by the largest and least precious of the boxes being of iron, which was rarely, if ever, used in Ramesside times, and was not common till the Greek age.

The magic engineering of Na.nefer.ka. ptah is very curious. The cabin or air-chamber of men in model, who are let down to work for him, suggests that Egyptians may have used the principle of a diving-bell or air-chamber for reaching parts under water. Certainly the device of raising things by dropping down sand to be put under them is still practised. An immense sarcophagus at Gizeh was raised from a deep well by natives who thrust sand under it rammed tight by a stick, and by this simple kind of hydraulic press raised it a hundred feet to the surface. In this way the magic men of Na.nefer.ka.ptah raised up the chest whenthey had discovered it by means of the sand which he poured over from the boat.

There is some picturesqueness in this tale, though it has not the charm of the earlier compositions. The scene of Ahura sitting for three days and nights, during the combat, watching by the side of the river, where she "had not drunk or eaten anything, and had done nothing on earth but sat like one who is gone to the grave," is a touching detail.

The light on the education of women is curious. Ahura can read the roll, but she cannot write. We are so accustomed to regard reading and writing as all one subject that the distinction is rare; but with a writing comprising so many hundred signs as the Egyptian, the art of writing or draw-Ing all the forms, and knowing which to use, is far more complex than that of reading. There are now ten students who can read an inscription for one who could compose it correctly. Here a woman of the highest rank is supposed to be able to read, but not to write;

that is reserved for the skill of "a good writer, and a very learned one."

The writing of spells and then washing the ink off and drinking it is a familiar idea in the East. Modern Egyptian bowls have charms engraved on them to be imparted to the drink, and ancient Babylonian bowls are inscribed with the like purpose.

An insight into the powers of the gods is here given us. The Egyptian did not attribute to them omniscience. Thoth only discovered what Na.nefer.ka.ptah had done as they were sailing away, some days after the seizure of the book. And even Ra is informed by the complaint of Thoth. If Ra were the physical sun it would be obvious that he would see all that was being done on earth; it would rather be he who would inform Thoth. The conception of the gods must therefore have been not pantheistic or materialist, but solely as spiritual powers who needed to obtain information, and who only could act through intermediaries. Further, nothing can be done without the consent of Ra; Thoth is powerless over men, and can only ask Ra, as a sort of universal magistrate, to take notice of the offence. Neither god acts directly, but by means of a power or angel, who takes the commission to work on men. How far this police-court conception of the gods is due to Greek or foreign influence can hardly be estimated yet. It certainly does not seem in accord with the earlier appeals to Ra, and direct action of Ra, in "Anpu and Bata."

The power of spells is limited, as we have just seen the abilities of the gods were limited. The most powerful of spells, the magic book of Thoth himself, cannot restore life to a person just drowned. All that Na. nefer.ka.ptah can do with the spell is to cause the body to float and to speak, but it remains so truly dead that it is buried as if no spell had been used. Now it was recognised that the ka could move about and speak to living persons, as Ahura does to Setna. Hence all that the spells do is not to alter the course of nature, but only to put the person into touch and communication with the ever-present supernatural, to enable him to know what the birds, the fishes, and the beasts all said, and to see the unseen.

Modern conceptions of the spiritual are so bound up with the sense of omnipresence and omniscience that we are apt to read those ideas into the gods and the magic of the ancients. Here we have to deal with gods who have to obtain information, and who order powers to act for them, with spells which extend the senses to the unseen, but which do not affect natural results and changes.

The inexorable fate in this tale which brings one after another of the family to die in the same spot is not due to Greek influence, though it seems akin to that. In the irrepressible transmigrations of Bata, and the successive risks of the Doomed Prince, the same ideas are seen working in the Egyptian mind. The remorse of Na.nefer.ka.ptah is a stronger touch of conscience and of shame than is seen in early times.

There is an unexplained point in the action as to how Na.nefer.ka.ptah, with the book upon him, comes up from the water, after he is drowned, into the cabin of the royal boat. The narrator had a difficulty to account for the recovery of the body without the use of the magic book, and so that stage is left unnoticed. The successive stages of embalming and mourning are detailed. The sixteen days in the Good House is probably the period of treatment of the body, the time up to the thirty-fifth day that of wrapping and decoration of the mummy cartonnage, and then the thirty-five days more of lying in state until the burial.

We now reach the third act, of Setna's struggle to get the magic roll. Here the strange episode comes in of the rival magicians gambling; it recalls the old tale of Rampsinitus descending into Hades and playing at dice with Ceres, and the frequent presence of draught-boards in the tombs, shows how much the ka was supposed to relish such pleasures. The regular Egyptian game-board had three rows of ten squares, or thirty in all. Such are found from the XIIth Dynasty down to Greek times; but this form has now entirely disappeared, and the man-galah of two rows of six holes, or the tab of four rows of nine holes, have taken its place. Both of these are side games, where different sides belong to opposite players. The commoner siga is a square game, five rows of five, or seven rows of seven holes, and has no personal sides. The ancient game was played with two, or perhaps three, different kinds of men, and the squares were counted from one end along the outer edge; but what the rules were, or how a game of fifty-two points was managed, has not yet been explained.

The strange scene of Setna being sunk into the ground portion by portion, as he loses successive games, is parallel to a mysterious story among the dervishes in Palestine. They tell how the three holy shekhs of the Dervish orders, Bedawi, Erfa'i, and Desuki, went in succession to Baghdad to ask for a jar of water of Paradise from the Derwisha Bint Bari, who seems to be a sky-genius, controlling the meteors. The last applicant, Desuki, was refused like the others; so he said, "Earth! swallow her," and the earth swallowed her to her knees; still she gave not the water, so he commanded the earth, and she was swallowed to her waist; a third time she refused, and she was swallowed to her breasts; she then asked him to marry her, which he would not; a fourth time she refused the water and was swallowed to her neck. She then ordered a servant to bring the water ("Palestine Exploration Statement, 1894," p. 32). The resemblance is most remarkable in two tales two thousand years apart; and the incident of Bint Bari asking the dervish to marry her has its connection with this tale. Had the dervish done so he would--according to Eastern beliefs--have lost his magic power over her, just as Setna loses his magic power by his alliance with Tabubua, to which he is tempted by Na.nefer.ka.ptah, in order to subdue him. The talisman here is a means of subduing magic powers, and is of more force than that of Thoth, as Ptah is greater than he.

The fourth act recounts the overcoming of the power of Setna by Na.nefer.ka.ptah, who causes Tabubua to lead to the loss of his superior magic, and thus to subdue him to the magic of his rival. Ankhtaui, here named as the place of Tabubua, was a quarter of Memphis, which is also named as the place of the wife of Uba-aner in the first tale.

The fifth act describes the victory of Na.nefer.ka.ptah, and his requiring Setna to reunite the family in his tomb at Memphis. The contrast between Ahura's pious ascription to Ptah, and her husband's chuckle at seeing his magic successful, is remarkable. Setna at once takes the position of an inferior by addressing praises to Na.nefer.ka.ptah: after which the tomb became bright as it was before he took away the magic roll. Setna then having made restitution, is required to give some compensation as well.

The search for the tomb of Ahura and Mer-ab is a most tantalising passage. The great cemetery of Koptos is the scene, and the search occupies three days and nights in the catacombs and on the steles. Further, the tomb was at the south corner of the town of Pehemato, as

Maspero doubtfully reads it. Yet this cemetery is now quite unknown, and in spite of all the searching of the native dealers, and the examination which I have made on the desert of both sides of the Nile, it is a mystery where the cemetery can be. The statement that the tomb was at the south corner of a town pretty well excludes it from the desert, which runs north and south there. And it seems as if it might have been in some raised land in the plain, like the spur or shoal on which the town of Koptos was built. If so it would have been covered by the ten to twenty feet rise of the Nile deposits since the time of its former use.

The appearance of the ancient to guide Setna gives some idea of the time that elapsed between then and the death of Ahura. The ancient, who must be allowed to represent two or three generations, says that his great-grandfather knew of the burial, which would take it back to five or six generations. This would place the death of Ahura about 150 years before the latter part of the reign of Ramessu II., say 1225 B.C.: thus, being taken back to about 1375 B.C., would make her belong to the generation after Amenhotep III., agreeing well with Mer.neb. ptah, being a corruption of the name of that king. No argument could be founded on so slight a basis; but at least there is no contradiction in the slight indications which we can glean.

The fear of Setna is that this apparition may have come to bring him into trouble by leading him to attack some property in this town; and Setna is particularly said to have restored the ground as it was before, after removing the bodies.

The colophon at the end is unhappily rather illegible. But the thirty-fifth year precludes its belonging to the reign of any Ptolemy, except the IInd or the VIIIth; and by the writing Maspero attributes it to the earlier of these reigns.